"It has been said by some that by emphasizing rewards we turn disciples into mercenaries. Tom Lancaster and writers of the New Testament would disagree! He shows us in this book that it takes great faith and hope to live for God's kingdom rewards. Tom wants to stir up the right kinds of desires for the right kind of rewards, not by a heavy application of the law but by pointing us to the glorious grace of God."

—Dean Wood, Pastor
Creekside Bible Church
Spring, TX

"Practicing architect Tom Lancaster does what those in his profession do best: combine form with function. He takes the beauty of the overarching purpose of the gospel of Jesus Christ (the part that compels us to follow) and draws our attention to the carefully crafted details that many of us miss. If you are a believer who has ever asked yourself the question, 'Now that I have eternal life, of what benefit is it to lead a righteous life?' This book will help."

—Steve Bradley, Pastor
StoneBridge Church
The Woodlands, TX

Most Christians think about eternal life as something that goes on forever in linear time. Of course this is true, but unbelievers also have an eternal life that continues forever. The difference between the two groups is not the *quantity* of existence, but the *quality* of existence. But that's not all. Tom Lancaster paints a beautiful portrait showing how the quality of eternal life for the believer can get better and better. With his gift for simplicity and clarity, he unpacks passage after passage in the New Testament showing us how one can improve the quality of eternal life by improving his walk with Christ today.

—David Anderson, Th.M., Ph.D.
President of Grace School of Theology

IMPROVING THE
QUALITY
OF YOUR
ETERNAL LIFE

A Primer on New Testament Exhortations to the Believer

THOMAS M. LANCASTER

Improving the Quality of Your Eternal Life

Copyright © 2016 by Thomas M. Lancaster

Published by Grace Theology Press.

All rights reserved. No part of this book may be reproduced in any form without permission in writing from the author, except in the case of brief quotations embodied in or reviews or in the case of using the material to teach on the subject.

All Scripture quotations, unless noted otherwise, are from The Holy Bible, New King James Version © 1982. New King James Version, New Testament and New Testament with Psalms © 1980, 1979 by Thomas Nelson Inc.

ISBN 10: 0-9965614-4-7
ISBN 13: 978-0-9965614-4-0
eISBN 10: 0-9965614-5-5
eISBN 13: 978-0-9965614-5-7

Special Sales: Most Grace Theology Press titles are available in special quantity discounts. Custom imprinting or excerpting can also be done to fit special needs. Contact Grace Theology Press at info@gracetheology.org.

Printed in the United States of America

TABLE OF CONTENTS

Acknowledgements vii

Preface 1

Chapter 1: The Lamb And The Judge 11

Chapter 2: The Called And The Chosen 21

Chapter 3: The First And The Last 31

Chapter 4: The Gift And The Inheritance 43

Chapter 5: Robes And Wedding Garments 55

Chapter 6: Confessing And Denying 67

Chapter 7: The Least And The Greatest 75

Chapter 8: Abiding And Burning 85

Epilogue 99

End Notes 103

Appendix A 123

Appendix B 126

ACKNOWLEDGEMENTS

First and foremost, I would to thank the Holy Spirit for guiding me as I have taken an exciting journey through the scriptures over the past four decades. Without reliance upon His insight and direction, no book of this sort would be possible.

Second, I would like to recognize teachers and professors who have not only been influential in my journey, but who have encouraged me to let the text speak for itself when it comes to interpretations of difficult passages. There are few thoughts expressed within the pages of this book that are truly original. For the most part, the content of this book has been inspired by the teaching and writing of men who have dedicated their lives to the study and proclamation of the Word of God. In this regard, I am very much indebted to Dr. Dave Anderson (Grace School of Theology) for his unswerving advocacy of "free grace" and his uncanny ability to turn Bible study into an adventure. I would also like to thank Dr. T. Kem Oberholtzer (Grace Rock Ministries) for his insight and encouragement.

Third, I am especially appreciative of my prison ministry team members, Glenn, Bob, John, Tex and Bruce, for the many hours of "fellowshipping in the Word" while driving to and from the Ferguson Unit in Midway, Texas over the past seven years. It has been a joy to wrestle with and explore the meaning, application and depth of God's word with such close friends.

Last, but by no means least, I would like to thank my wonderful wife, who first introduced me to the gospel 41 years ago; and without whose persistence early in our relationship I might never have become saved.

PREFACE

Some may find the title of this book intriguing, if not preposterous or incredible. Isn't life in eternity (at least once we are freed from our sin nature) supposed to be perfect? How then can its quality be improved? Moreover, even if a believer could presume to effect such a change, how would he do it? As unfamiliar as this may be to some, the concept of contributing to the quality of one's eternal life is a significant topic in the New Testament. It is repeatedly mentioned by Jesus and is a frequent concern of the writers of the epistles.

The ability to *contribute to the quality of* eternal life, however, must be distinguished from *gaining* eternal life. Gaining eternal life is acquired only by placing one's trust in the work of Jesus on the cross, for justification is gained by faith alone. Contributing to the quality of eternal life, on the other hand, can only occur *after* one becomes justified; and is directly linked to paying the cost of discipleship, or "running the race with endurance".

So important is the abundant aspect of eternal life that Jesus exhorts His followers to contribute towards it at any opportunity, using every worldly resource at their disposal. This is the essential meaning of the parable of the "unjust steward" in Luke 16:1-9. Here Jesus tells of a steward who, having just learned of his imminent firing and not wanting to be forced into manual labor, sets out to create friends in the business world by reducing their indebtedness to his master. Upon learning of his steward's actions, the master, though still releasing his steward, commends him for his shrewdness. In applying the parable, Jesus says, *"For the sons of this world are more shrewd in their generation than the sons of light. And I say to you, make friends for yourselves by unrighteous mammon, that when you fail, they may receive you into an everlasting kingdom."* Jesus points out that unbelievers (sons of this world) are quite adept and clever at using worldly resources to lay up for themselves so that they may enjoy the later years of their lives. As a mild rebuke, Jesus says that believers (sons of light) are typically far less dedicated in using their worldly resources (unrighteous mammon) to lay up for themselves so they may have an *abundant eternal life*. His rebuke is magnified when one realizes that the "sons of the world" are laying up that which will perish; while the "sons of light" have the opportunity to lay up what can never be destroyed! The subjects of the chapters of this book derive from Jesus' voiced concern in the parable of the unjust steward.

It seems evident from Scripture that there is a hierarchy among believers in the coming kingdom. This ranking stems from the devotedness of disciples, and has application to all believers. In running our individual "races", we might ask ourselves: Are we living with the expectation that we will someday face Jesus, who will judge all that we have used in building on the foundation He has laid? (Ch. 1) Are we responding to the divine call in our lives? (Ch. 2) Do we love Christ more than all else in this world? (Ch. 3) Are we investing our lives in things of eternal value? (Ch. 4) Are we earnestly preparing to meet our groom? (Ch. 5) Do we openly confess Jesus and the gospel message by the way we live? (Ch. 6) Are we making the gospel attractive to others, or do we bring offense to the name of Jesus? (Ch. 7) Are we abiding in Jesus and bearing fruit? (Ch. 8)

The chapter titles contain the familiar terminology used in the gospels and epistles that refer to the above questions. The driving force behind the writing of this book was a desire to address the misunderstanding of these familiar terms and Bible passages. It began a number of years back when I was given the opportunity to teach the adult Sunday school class I regularly attend. Our instructor, a seminary professor with a Th.D. in Bible Exposition from Dallas Theological Seminary, planned to be gone one Sunday, and our normal back-up teacher was scheduled to be absent on the same date. With two weeks advance notice, I pondered what topic I might address for a single session that would challenge our astute class. Having just spent some time reading in the gospel of Matthew, I decided to teach on the topic of "outer darkness[1] where there is weeping and gnashing of teeth," an odd expression that has puzzled a number of Bible commentators.

My initial research focused on the "Parable of the Marriage Feast" in Matthew 22:1-14, in which "outer darkness" is found. In an online search, I found two essays written specifically on the passage, one by Gregory Sapaugh and the other by Hampton Keithley IV, offering opposing interpretations. As I researched further, it became apparent that the clues to understanding the parable's meaning were scattered in passages throughout both the Old and New Testaments. These passages frequently contained serious warnings to *believers*. The interpretations of these warnings, as with that of the "outer darkness" passages, are controversial among scholars, and few commentaries agree with the conclusions to be presented in this text. It was also apparent there was widespread disagreement on the concept of "free grace", the role of works in a believer's life, and the judgment seat of Christ. Further study revealed that some positions on these topics could not be supported from scripture; while others were either inconsistent or confusing.

These issues are precisely those that arise in the Lord's letter to the church in Laodicea mentioned in Revelation 3:14-22. Its believing members seem to have taken the grace of God for granted: their doctrine had become polluted; their lives were entangled in the world; they had become self-reliant instead of God-reliant; they were in need of repentance, and had become blind to their spiritually-wretched condition. Incredibly, Jesus pictures Himself outside the church, hoping someone with "ears to hear" will open the door to his repeated knocking. Could it be that the Laodicean church is mirrored in this current generation of American Christians?

It is not as if the corruption of the Church at the end of this age should be a surprise. This carnal tendency of the "kingdom in the absence of the King" was foretold by Jesus in several of the parables in Matthew 13. In the parable of the wheat and the weeds (13:24-30, 36-43), for example, it is apparent that some believers in the world become so entangled with "things that cause sin" that the harvesters are forbidden to remove the weeds until the end of the age, lest those members be "uprooted" as well! In the parable of the mustard seen (13:31-32) the agents of Satan ("birds of the air"[2]) nest in "visible Christendom", which has grown unpruned[3] in the world. And in the parable of the leaven (13:33-34) "visible Christendom" becomes filled with hypocrisy.[4]

The parables in Matthew 13 and the letter to the Laodicean church raise several important questions. What does God do with a believer who falls into a carnal, fruitless and destructive lifestyle? What does He do with a person whose actions may even work against the advancement of the kingdom of God after he has trusted in Christ? Does that person lose his salvation? Do his worldly lifestyle and lack of good works indicate he was never a believer to begin with? Can a believer "fall away from grace" and still retain eternal life? What if a believer chooses not to believe any longer? <u>Though all believers are Christ's workmanship (Ephesians 2:10), the outcome is not predetermined; nor does it follow that all believers will have lives that are significantly transformed.</u> For all of us, the outcome is dependent on the yielding of our will and the subduing of our flesh as we submit to the shaping hands of the Potter.

About the same time as my opportunity to teach on "outer darkness," two of the employees at my architectural firm entered into a discussion over eternal security. One of them adamantly believed a Christian could lose his salvation by backsliding in his faith. When I offered an opposing view on the subject, he could not adequately defend his position, and directed me to a website dedicated to proving that eternal security was a heretical doctrine. In hopes of correcting my employee's view of eternal life (and of God), I visited the website he suggested. I was not prepared for what I encountered. Page after page of Bible verses were used to assert one could lose his salvation. I had expected that the arguments against eternal security would be based on a few problematic passages from scripture, but instead found myself confronted with a host of verses whose true meaning I never dreamed could be twisted.

I observed that the misinterpretations found on the website were the result of a failure to recognize several important truths about the New Testament:

- For the most part, the epistles were written to address lifestyle and doctrinal issues in the early church. It was not the authors' intent to save their readers' *souls*, but to save their *earthly lives*, so that they might someday stand blameless at the judgment seat of Christ. Even in the gospels, there is a distinct emphasis on discipleship.[5] Among the books of the New Testament, the gospel of John is perhaps the only one with a purely evangelistic intent (see John 20:30-31). Therefore, the subject at hand when encountering New Testament passages that warn believers is typically *sanctification*, not justification.

- Related to a believer's sanctification, the quality of one's fellowship with God, the depth of one's love of God, and the fruitfulness of "abiding in Christ" are frequent topics in the epistles. But broken fellowship, waning love and failure to abide do not threaten one's justification any more than a son's waywardness threatens to alter the DNA he acquired from his parents. Similarly, God's discipline and wrath are not the same as the exercise of His justice. The former (wrath) is almost always temporal; and when applied to a believer, is used to bring about repentance, renewed love and restored fellowship. The latter (justice) has already been taken care of for all believers, since Jesus bore in his body the "just" penalty for our sins.

- The self-evident truth about eternal life is that it is *eternal*. If Jesus offers eternal life, how then can it be lost or given back? If eternal life can be lost or given back, or if it is dependent upon performance, obedience, continued faith or ritual, then, by definition, it was not *eternal* to begin with . . . and Jesus' promise was false. Surely, "conditional eternal life" (for such it should be called) is an oxymoronic term.

"Perseverance justification" is the false notion that a person must be faithful (persevere) in his walk with Christ to the end of his life in order to have eternal life (be justified). Under this view, a believer's failure to endure in his walk might indicate either: 1) having never been saved to begin with, or 2) no longer believing in the gospel and forfeiting the salvation previously granted. In neither of these two suppositions is there assurance of eternal life after placing one's faith in the death and resurrection of Jesus Christ; for in the first case justification must be *proven* by the believer and in the second it must be *maintained* by him.

Standing in stark contrast to this position is "free grace,"[6] emphasized by Paul in Romans 5. Under this position,

Preface

justification is by *faith alone in Christ alone*; totally independent of evidence of change in a person's lifestyle or the extent to which he produces righteous works. Justification cannot be earned, deserved, maintained or lost by the believer; and requires of him no proof or contribution. It is free; being totally secured by Christ's death on the cross.

The usual complaint against free grace, made by those who believe in "perseverance justification," is the assumption that a believer can sin all he wants if he knows he cannot lose his salvation. Technically, of course, a believer *can* sin all he wants. This is precisely the reason for Paul's questions in Romans 6:1 and 6:15. He was acutely aware that the "free grace" he proclaimed in Romans 5:15-21 could be abused . . . and at the same time adamant that justification *could not be lost* as a result! He says in 5:20b, *"But where sin abounded, grace abounded much more."* With regard to justification, Paul says a believer cannot sin beyond the coverage of God's grace.

Those who deny free grace tend to overlook the restraining effect of conviction of the Holy Spirit in a believer's life and the disciplinary action of God, which can be quite severe.[7] But worse than this is the failure to see the legalistic and ungrateful view of God that springs from such a denial, as well as an envious attitude toward "free grace" adherents.

The primary restraint to a sinful lifestyle (for those of us who believe in eternal security) is thankfulness to God for having been <u>eternally</u> saved. We realize the full extent to which we were lost, and the full measure of God's forgiveness (of all past, present and future sins). Regarding the harlot who wiped His feet with her hair and her tears, Jesus said (in effect), *"This woman loves Me much because she realizes she has been forgiven much. But he who has been forgiven little, loves little."* (Luke 7:47) There is a direct proportional relationship between realized forgiveness and the depth of one's love of God.

A person who does not fully know whether he is saved or not until the day he dies cannot be said to have lived a life in full appreciation of God's forgiveness, for he has lived as if his justification has always been dependent on his obedience. Since it is up to him to "maintain" his justification, the extent of his appreciation of Christ's work at the cross is necessarily diminished. *Love for God* becomes *obligation to God*. Denial of free grace will thus rob a believer of joyful fellowship with Jesus, and of the abundant blessings He wants to bestow, both in this age and the next.

Looking at God through the legalistic glasses of "perseverance justification" distorts the meaning of many passages in the New Testament, particularly those referring to the judgment seat of Christ and the Millennium. Since the Biblical principle of free grace is so intricately woven into the fabric of the gospels and epistles, these distortions can become quite significant and widespread.

The idea that a believer can lose his salvation springs, in part, from the significant amount of worldliness observed within the congregations of America's churches. It is as if those holding to a "perseverance justification" want desperately to show the unbelieving world that the true Church is different. In an attempt to keep it on the right path, they turn grace into an ugly concept, where a believer's eternal status is judged by external evidences (his works before men). This has the unfortunate consequence of turning believers into "spiritual fruit inspectors." While a believer's justification is unaffected by future sinful behavior, there is a serious question to be answered: If a carnal believer does not lose his salvation, what consequences are there, other than a return to slavery to sin?[8] And are these consequences temporal (experienced only in this life); or do they have a more far-reaching impact (experienced in the next age or into eternity)?

As for temporal consequences, it cannot be said that God ignores a lifestyle of sin in one of His own. He is continually active in His discipline of those who have been adopted into His family. *"For whom the Lord loves He chastens, and scourges every son whom He receives."* (Hebrews 12:6) But as much as the New Testament writers (and more importantly God, who inspired them) are concerned with the temporal impact of sin in a believer's life and God's corrective discipline, they are equally concerned with the consequences in the age to come. For God desires a much deeper relationship with every believer than we can possibly imagine . . . and how much does He want this in eternity as well as the present! Since there is a direct correlation between faithfulness in this life and the depth of one's relationship with God in the next, the warnings to believers in the New Testament must be understood accordingly. The *quality* of one's eternal life hangs in the balance.

If not the loss of justification, what then are the far-reaching consequences of a life lived carnally by a believer? How do they differ from the consequences of a life lived faithfully? *Can the quality of eternal life be improved by the choices a believer makes in this life?* The following chapters are meant to answer these questions using scripture and familiar illustrations from everyday life. The interpretations of the numerous passages quoted in these chapters may not be familiar, and it is my prayer that the reader will be both challenged and enlightened as he reads; with hope that he will gain a new understanding and appreciation of scripture, and ultimately be drawn into a deeper relationship with God.

Tom Lancaster
The Woodlands, Texas

1

THE LAMB AND THE JUDGE

It would be hard to miss the spiritual decline in America today. At the core of this decline is a departure from true doctrines of the Christian faith in America's churches; a sad characteristic directly proportional to the Biblically illiteracy of our congregations. The apostle Paul would warn his readers not to be "children" subject to being *"tossed to and fro and carried about with every wind of doctrine . . ."* but to *". . . grow up in all things into Him who is the head – Christ . . ."* (Ephesians 4:14-15).

Drifting from true doctrine is the result of the Church having lost a sense of its calling; its direction and purpose. Instead of being "salt" and "light," churches in America have succumbed to the political correctness of our day. Friendliness with the world has become the default strategy for church growth; and filling pews has become a higher priority than developing the spiritual maturity of the congregation. I suspect a number of Biblical topics are left unaddressed from the pulpit and in Sunday school classes because their introduction might offend members or make them uncomfortable. As a consequence of this sort of political correctness congregations are not exposed to the deeper spiritual truths of the Bible. Sermon topics can become superficial, emphasizing the loving attributes of God while minimizing the more difficult topics that address His holiness and perfect justice.

Over-emphasis of the Lamb

Recently, I volunteered to teach a first grade boys' Sunday school class in my own church. This proved, at first, to be a challenge, since it had been a number of years since I had been involved in anything but adult level discussions in my Christian education and teaching. I knew that making spiritual truths relevant to six year-olds would require an entirely different approach. The curriculum I was given to use was written by a well-known Christian publisher. It contained thirteen lessons, each with a different focus. After my first four classes, it seemed as if I was teaching nearly the same principles each Sunday. Both the boys' level of interest and mine began to wane. Frustrated, I scanned the remaining nine lessons and discovered my suspicions of "sameness" were correct. Every lesson focus was limited to illustrating God's love or kindness. Four lessons in succession dealt with God's kindness, the child's desire to be kind, the child's ability to be kind to others, and how God could help him be kind; representing over five consecutive hours of "kindness" stories, games, role playing, and other activities. <u>Not one lesson in the entire 13-week curriculum dealt with sin, its consequences or its remedies.</u> While we should be sensitive to the topics introduced to six year-olds, the idea that God judges sin is not one of them.

Adult education can often fall into the same harmless, inoffensive, "God-is-love" routine. If classes such as "Finding

Christian Themes in Hollywood Movies," "The Canonization of the Bible," and "Developing Your Storytelling Skills" are not balanced by verse-by-verse studies of the word of God, the maturity of a congregation will become severely ill-equipped to deal with the "trickery of men and cunning craftiness of deceitful plotting" Paul mentions in Ephesians 4:14.

The tendency to over-emphasize the gentle, meek and lamb-like image of Jesus has overshadowed the terrifying image of Him that caused the apostle John to fall down as if dead (Revelation 1:13-17), and obscured the real meaning of many warning passages to the casual reader of the New Testament. When Jesus says in Matthew 10:37, *"He who loves son or daughter more than Me is not worthy of Me,"* and in 10:39, *"He who finds his life will lose it, and he who loses his life for My sake will find it,"* He is not contrasting believers with unbelievers. The context clearly shows He is discussing discipleship: what one does with his life <u>after</u> he has believed unto salvation. Jesus is contrasting committed disciples with uncommitted disciples. He is seeking disciples who will pay the necessary cost to follow Him. The willingness to forsake all was perhaps the most important trait Jesus sought for in the twelve He chose to follow Him. It is likely no different today.

Eschatology and the goal of the believer

The goal of a believer's life is not met in becoming justified, for placing one's trust in Jesus merely establishes the starting point. Rather, the goal of Christianity is to "run the race with endurance." It is a measure of our thankfulness for the priceless gift of eternal life that we "pick up our cross" to follow Jesus. Failure to pursue Jesus with abandon, forsaking the world, indicates not only a lack of thankfulness, but a poor understanding of the consequences of such a choice. Such consequences can be realized in this age, and surely will be in the next.

The church has lost sight of this goal, in part, due to a departure from correct eschatology. Largely from Augustine's influence in the fourth century A.D., the Roman Catholic Church and many protestant churches today no longer separate the judgment seat[1] of Christ for *believers* (1 Cor. 3:11-15, 2 Cor. 5:10) from the great white throne judgment for *unbelievers* (Rev. 20:11-15). In both events individuals are judged for their works. In neither case, however, is the issue of eternal life at stake, for it has already been determined. Those who appear at the judgment seat of Christ have already been justified[2], and those who appear at the great white throne judgment stand condemned.[3] The purpose in judging works for the believer is to determine the level of privileges (service, responsibility, etc.) in the age to come, while the purpose in judging works for the unbeliever is perhaps to determine the level of eternal punishment. (See the Prophetic Timetable at the end of this chapter.) Serious errors in the interpretation of many New Testament passages will necessarily result if these two judgment events are lumped together: 1) Free grace will become supplanted by a works justification[4], and 2) The emphasis on sanctification found in most of the NT epistles will be distorted.[5]

The danger of disqualification

In my high school days, almost anyone could be on the track team, for football was the king of sports in Texas. Our track coach welcomed to the team everyone that showed up. Being on the team, however, did not earn one a letter jacket. To gain sufficient points to letter in track in a running event, one had to spend hours on end after school and on weekends running scheduled distances designed to train him for a specific race. The coach would analyze each runner's giftedness and place him in events that were most likely to benefit the team. If a team member worked hard, it usually benefitted the entire team at track meets. However, if one didn't run on weekends and didn't give full effort at practices, just the opposite occurred: he hurt the team's chances of winning a meet. The consequence of laziness was a shamefully-run race before spectators, as well as the coach. Repeated poor performances would earn a team member demotion or "disqualification" from events, or a position on a relay team. This is exactly the imagery used by the apostle Paul in 1 Corinthians 9:27, where he says, *"But I discipline my body and bring it into subjection, lest, when I have preached to others, I myself should become disqualified."*

Who is it that does the disqualifying? It is the Lord Jesus, before whom every believer will give an account of his life after being saved.[6] This alarming view of Jesus is confirmed by Paul in 2 Corinthians 5:10 – *"For we must all appear before the judgment seat of Christ, that each one may receive the things done in the body,* according to what he has done, whether good or bad." The "good" aspects of this judgment are somewhat familiar to many Christians, but the "bad" aspects are usually ignored, denied altogether, or erroneously relegated to non-believers. It is clear from scripture, however, that there will be bad consequences for some believers at the judgment seat of Christ, which may last into the Millennium and perhaps into eternity. These bad consequences appear to be in direct relation to the "bad" (**kakos** – worthless, of no value) things done while *"in the body."*

And what is it that Paul feared disqualification from? It was disqualification from all of the privileges that would otherwise have been granted to a believer who had served Christ faithfully during his life. These privileges may last the entirety of the Millennium. Paul certainly did not fear disqualification from eternal life (justification), for he makes it clear that justification is not earned or merited, and that salvation does not rely in any way on works (Ephesians 2:8-9).

On a sports team, "disqualification" happens when coach loses confidence in an athlete's abilities or dedication to winning. The loss of confidence is coupled with a loss of opportunity to contribute to the cause of the team in the future, a loss of the thrill of "being in the game", and of the joy of bringing glory to one's alma mater. Disqualification can also come with the voiced displeasure of the coach; and no athlete wants to face a coach who feels his time has been wasted.

The danger of drifting

The book of Hebrews warns believers against "drifting" in their faith, and describes the consequences of a continued downward slide, where one's heart becomes hardened to the process of sanctification. The warnings in this book are controversial, and as mentioned previously, are often used wrongly to convey the idea that a Christian can lose his salvation, or that a Christian who hardens his heart to God's leading was never a believer to begin with. Some do not like the portrayal of God as an "angry coach," but those who have trained as athletes will have no problem picturing the alarming images contained in Hebrews.

The plain message of Hebrews chapter 10 is this: God has forever taken care of the sin that separated us from Him by the once-for-all, free-gift sacrifice of Jesus. To help us mature in our faith, we have received another free gift; that of the Holy Spirit that indwells our hearts. Therefore, seeing all that God has done for us, we should <u>draw near with a true heart</u> (10:22), <u>hold fast to the confession of our hope</u> (10:23), <u>and exhort one another unto love and good works</u> (10:24). The verses that follow indicate the consequences of a believer's failure to appreciate the free gifts of God.

> *"For if we sin willfully after we have received the knowledge of the truth, there no longer remains a sacrifice for sins, but a fearful expectation of judgment, and fiery indignation which will devour the adversaries.*⁷*"* (10:26-27)
>
> *"Of how much worse punishment* [than dying without mercy for rejecting the law of Moses], *do you suppose,*

will he be thought worthy who has trampled the Son of God underfoot, counted the blood of the covenant by which he was sanctified a common thing, and insulted the Spirit of grace? (10:29)

"For we know Him who said, 'Vengeance is Mine, I will repay,' Says the Lord. And again, 'The Lord will judge His people.' It is a fearful thing to fall into the hands of the living God." (10:30-31)

There can be no question that the subjects being addressed are believers. The "we" includes the author as well as his readers. They have received (***lambanō*** = laid hold of) the knowledge (***epignoskō*** = full knowledge) of the truth; and have been sanctified (***hagiazō*** = free from guilt of sin) by the blood of the covenant.

Furthermore, only a believer can "insult the Spirit of grace," a condition undoubtedly worse than grieving the Holy Spirit,[8] and which speaks of abusing the grace one has already been given. Finally, the Lord is judging *"His people"*: not a term that would indicate unbelievers.

Note that the "fiery *indignation*" of 10:27 is not "fiery *condemnation.*" This corresponds directly to "being saved, yet so as through fire" in 1 Corinthians 3:15 at the judgment seat of Christ. That there "no longer remains a sacrifice for sins" (10:27) speaks of broken fellowship, not loss of eternal life. It is possible that the Jewish people to whom the author is writing were drifting from the Christian faith back into the Mosaic system, where there was no sacrifice that covered presumptuous sin.[9] Obedience to the Mosaic Law kept the nation of Israel in fellowship with God, and was a measure of their love for God. It was never intended as an instrument by which men could be justified, for justification is by faith alone.[10] The warning of Hebrews 10:26-31 is that God will severely penalize believers who willfully live a life of sin. Such a great gift as God's grace should be accepted with reverence and fear, *"for our God is a consuming fire."* (Hebrews 12:28-29)[11]

Paul uses even more severe language in 1 Corinthians 3:16-17: *"Do you not know that you are the temple of God and that the Spirit of God dwells in you? If anyone <u>defiles</u> the temple of God, God will <u>destroy</u> him. For the temple of God is holy, which temple you are."* (NKJV) The use of the word "destroy" in the NKJV is unfortunate, since it is the same Greek word **phthlirō**, properly translated "defile" in the same sentence. Paul warns the believer that defilement of his temple here on earth will cause similar defilement of his *reward in heaven*. There is no reference here to the loss of eternal life. Accordingly, he told the Philippians *". . . work out your own salvation with fear and trembling; for it is God who works in you both to will and to do for His good pleasure."* (Philippians 2:12-13)

The danger of losing one's witness

The believer who rejects the upward call of God in his life is all but useless to the plan and program of God. Jesus put it this way, regarding discipleship: *"Salt is good; but if the salt has lost its flavor, how shall it be seasoned? It is neither fit for the land nor for the dunghill, but men throw it out. He who has ears to hear, let him hear!"* (Luke 14:34-35) In the gospel of Matthew, Jesus makes a similar statement, also in the context of discipleship:[12] *"You are the salt of the earth; but if the salt loses its flavor, how shall it be seasoned? It is then good for nothing but to be thrown out and trampled underfoot by men."* (Matthew 5:13)

I assist in teaching in a prison ministry at a high-security unit once a week. The vast majority of those in this prison have committed violent crimes, and the prison itself can be a dangerous place for some inmates, especially if they refuse membership in one of the established gangs. This prompted us to ask the prisoners in our Bible class, "Do you ever get persecuted, or worry about attacks from other inmates for your faith in Jesus?" One of the older prisoners responded, "Actually, we are not bothered much. Most of the inmates here have already committed serious crimes, and perhaps they fear God's additional judgment if they were to do something to believers." He thought a second, then added, "However, if you say you are a Christian, and then act like an unbeliever; they will not hesitate to make you a target."

The average believing prisoner may well have a level of understanding of "flavorless salt" surpassing that of the average church-going Christian. A number of them have testified they knew the Lord before they landed in prison; and they are grateful to this day that God brought them to repentance. These inmates are now laying up treasure in heaven as they live behind bars; and are running the race with endurance. Most importantly, they have no illusions that "coach" Jesus will greet them with a "Well done, good and faithful servant" if they become lazy after having made the team. They are well aware of the consequences of their walk, both in this life and in the next age. Would it be so for all believers!

Summary

When Jesus came to earth the first time, He did not come to condemn,[13] but to serve, and to save sinners by dying on the cross. For almost 2,000 years He has interceded for believers before the Father. Someday, Jesus will judge each believer for how he lived his life after becoming saved. Meekness, mildness and gentleness would not be adequate descriptive terms for Jesus on that day. We will not come before a lamb, but a judge.

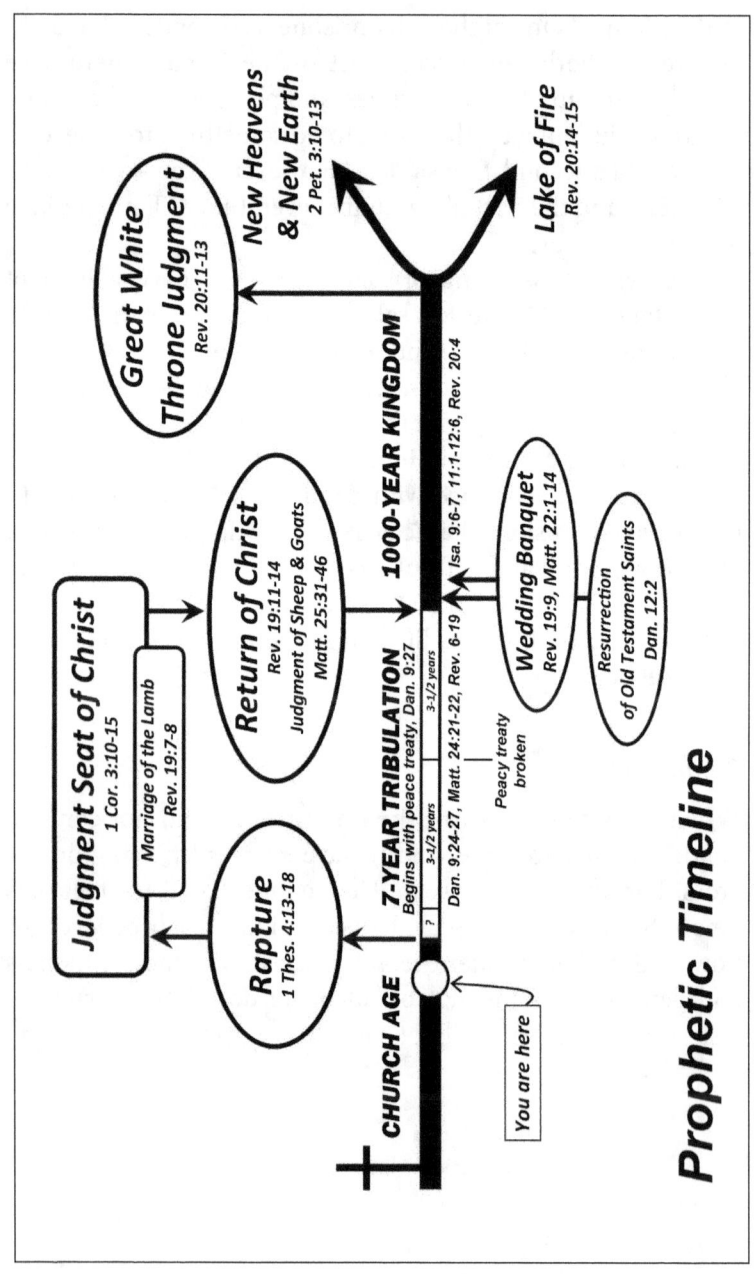

2

THE CALLED AND THE CHOSEN

The "earthly aspects" of the Millennium[1] to come are rarely discussed in adult Sunday school classes, and almost entirely ignored in the Christian education of children. Yet a believer's life is meant to prepare him for reigning with Christ <u>on the earth</u> during that age. Beyond the Millennium, the believer's eternal existence is also an <u>earthly</u> one; albeit on a new earth (Revelation 21:1). But many have been captivated by the imagery of an ethereal, dream-like abode where all sins are forgotten, everyone is joyful, and people in white robes walk across clouds. Nothing could be further from the truth about the next age. The Millennium will follow the Tribulation period, a time characterized by extensive destruction. There will be ruined cities to be re-built,[2] roads and infrastructure to be repaired, governments to establish,[3] and vast areas of the earth to be re-inhabited.[4]

If Jesus happened to place an ad in the local newspaper for the various administrative positions needed to help Him rule during the Millennium, I imagine it would look something like this:

> **JOB POSTING:** Openings available for qualified believers to help rule the coming kingdom. Resumé must indicate humility, trustworthiness, faithfulness, desire to serve others, selflessness, and willingness to confess Christ in the face of persecution. Unlimited benefits, exciting travel, executive dining and throne room privileges, 1,000-yr. job security, work directly with CEO, fulfilling and joyful work. This is a once-in-a-lifetime opportunity.

Life as a training ground

As parents, we encourage our children to strive to do their best in all they undertake. Our goal is to train, educate and equip them so that they will grow into maturity. We want each of them to be able to discern between truth and falsehood, to be able to handle responsibility, to become worthy of trust, and find their place as a productive member of society. For many, this includes the privilege of getting a college education. Many are grateful for this privilege and use it wisely. Some are less thankful, and do the minimum to get by. And unfortunately, some misspend this opportunity by drinking, partying and sleeping the hours away; accounting for millions of wasted dollars each year in this country. But more unfortunate than the wasted money from hard-working parents, charitable scholarships and government grants are the lost opportunities for employment in meaningful and rewarding professions. Futures are altered or thrown away without a second thought . . . forfeited to someone more deserving. It doesn't take much imagination to picture the confrontation that follows: "Son, what were you thinking? What did you do with the precious gift from your mother and me? How could you do this?"

As the owner of a small architectural firm I can testify of the poorly-written resumes that come across my desk, and the occasional ill-prepared applicant that sits at my conference table for an interview. The questions that come to my mind are: What did this applicant do with his time in college? Is he capable of learning my business? Will he dedicate himself each day to making my firm a success? Will he help it become more profitable? If he was not faithful with his opportunity to get an education, how can I expect him to be faithful in the more important responsibilities of designing a building? If he has put himself first up to this point in his life, or has done the minimum to get by, what reason do I have for thinking he will put the company first when he is my employee? Valuable opportunities are gained and lost by the answers to these questions. While irresponsible behavior in college might simply put one on probation, it can cause much more serious problems in the real world, where life safety is often at stake.

If the Church is to help Jesus rule the nations[5] during the Millennium, there will be an entire hierarchy of positions to fill, each one requiring a loyal, reliable, selfless and trustworthy candidate. Jesus' parable in Luke 19:11-27 indicates that servants with these character traits would be rewarded with authority over cities when He returned to set up His kingdom; some servants being given greater authority than others. Those servants who did not exhibit these character traits would forfeit the reward they could have had, since they were deemed not fit to rule.

The way a believer lives his present life will dictate his rewards (or loss of same) in the next age. Jesus graciously has purchased our lives in this age with His own life, and equipped us for our individual calling with the Holy Spirit. Some, having used their time wisely, will receive His commendation of *"Well done, good and faithful servant; you were faithful over a few things, I will make you ruler over many things. Enter into the joy of your lord."*[6] Others, having shamefully wasted their opportunity, will hear the equivalent of, "What were you thinking? "What did you do with my great and precious gift?"

The opportunity of divine appointment

It is in the context of devoted and faithful servants that Jesus warns twice in the gospel of Matthew that *"Many are called, but few are chosen."*[7] Jesus is not referring to "saved" (chosen) vs. "lost" (called but not chosen) individuals, but to <u>contrasting types of born-again believers</u>. The Greek word for "called" **(klētos)** in the above phrase means to be divinely selected or appointed, and in instances where it is found in the New Testament, it refers to *believers*. It should not be interpreted the same as **kaleō** (also meaning "called"), where a sinner can be "called" to repentance (Mark 2:17), or a believer "called" from darkness into light (1 Peter 2:9).

It might be said that **klētos** represents the ultimate reward that God desires to bestow on a believer, and the goal toward which his life should be aimed. It is used by Paul when he says he was <u>called</u> to be an apostle of Jesus Christ by the will of God (1Cor. 1:1). It is also used in Romans 8:28, where we find that *"all things work together for good to those who love God, to those who are <u>the called</u> according to His purpose."*

The divine appointments to which God calls believers should be understood not only in His calling for us in this life, but in His calling for us in the age to come. To the degree we attain to the former, the latter will be our reward in the kingdom. Accordingly, Paul writes in Philippians 3:14 that *"I press toward the mark for the prize of the high calling **(klēsis)** of God in Christ Jesus."* Paul's desire was to grow into the divine position that God had set before him as a prize, or reward. This is a position which is awarded only to a faithful disciple. It is an opportunity made available by faith in Christ's death and resurrection, but its realization is not guaranteed. The hard work of a disciple is required in this life to be found worthy of it, as Paul says to the church in Thessalonica:

> *"Therefore we also pray always for you that our God would count you worthy of this calling (**klēsis**), and fulfill all the good pleasure of His goodness and the work of faith with power . . ."* (2 Thessalonians 1:11)

Similarly, Peter emphasizes the need to press forward when he writes,

> *"Therefore, brethren, be even more diligent to* <u>make you call</u> *(**klēsis**)* <u>and election sure</u>, *for if you do these things, you will never stumble; for so an entrance will be supplied to you abundantly into the everlasting kingdom of our Lord and Savior Jesus Christ."* (2 Peter 1:10)

Both "called" and "chosen" are illustrated in the above passage. Peter wants his readers to ensure that they are found worthy and *chosen* (elected) for that to which they have been *called*, which is an *abundant* entrance into the kingdom. And how can they ensure they are found worthy? By being diligent in this life to do the things Peter lists in 1:5-9. These verses should not be interpreted to mean "ensuring one's justification", for gaining eternal life does not depend on one's diligence. The essence of free grace is that *no one* is worthy of eternal life.

Looking for a few good men

If the "called" (***klētos***) in Matthew 20:16 and 22:14 are believers, then what is the significance of being "chosen"? The word "chosen" (***eklektos***) is used in the New Testament to refer primarily to the Church, which is <u>chosen out of the world</u>. Yet the use of ***eklektos*** to apply to individuals in the two passages in Matthew indicates <u>choosing from among believers</u>. This is also the meaning suggested by the surrounding context (Matthew 20:1-16), where the vineyard owner rewards a *chosen* group of workers, and the king (Matthew 22:1-14) grants a place at his banquet only for a *chosen* group of those invited to come.[9]

My wife has taught ballet to high school students for over 35 years. The studio she currently works for performs the Nutcracker ballet every year before Christmas. I know from her that the various dancing roles in the ballet are earned by merit; each performer having to audition for the role. The most significant roles are given to the most talented and hard-working dancers, while the least significant roles are given to those with little experience, less talent, or less desire to improve their dancing ability. Most often, the lead role of the Sugar Plum Fairy is awarded to a senior in high school, but on occasion would go to a younger, more talented girl. Due to the difficult level of the choreography, the desire to show off the teaching capability of the studio, and the need to entertain a paying audience, selecting well-qualified dancers for major roles is important. One would not entertain the thought of promoting a dancer to a prominent role for which she is incapable.

This common-sense principle has an eternal application. Though all believers are appointed for preordained tasks or roles, many do not (and will not) reach their potential. Believers are not equal in their works, their trustworthiness, or their faithfulness. A distinction is made throughout the New Testament between those who merely believe and those who, having believed, grow into maturity, endure, and overcome. Believers are therefore *called* (***klētos***) unto holiness (1 Corinthians 1:2) and *called* (***klētos***) to seek the power of God unto sanctification (1 Corinthians 1:24). Scripture indicates that God will chose from among the "called" at the judgment seat of Christ.

Rewards of the chosen

This distinction between "called" and "chosen" is evident in 2 Timothy 2:11b-12a: *"For if we died with Him* [all believers], *we shall also live with Him. If we endure* [only believers who persevere in their walk], *we shall also reign with Him."*[8] It is evident that those who are <u>chosen to reign</u> in the Millennial kingdom are believers who endure in their faith, who demonstrate (in this life) the capability of handling their Lord's estate; whose devotion is un-affected by trials and persecution, and the cares and allures of this world. They will enjoy a closer relationship with Jesus and given greater responsibility. *They will be more than mere residents in the kingdom.*

This is a recurrent theme in the letters to the churches in Revelation 2 and 3. Those who "overcome," "hold fast," and "persevere" are promised a number of rights and privileges. They will be granted the right to eat from the tree of life (2:7), given a crown of life (2:10), given a white stone and a "new name" known only to the individual and Jesus" (2:17), given the privilege of ruling with Christ (2:26), given the morning star (2:28), given the privilege of walking with Jesus in white garments (3:5), made "pillars" in the temple of God, with their names written thereupon (3:12), and given the privilege of dining with Jesus along with sitting on the Father's throne (3:21). *These are all rewards based on faithful service*, and all indicate a closer fellowship with Jesus in eternity will be experienced as a result.

Increasing the performance of the believer

Each of the two parables in which the phrase "many are called but few are chosen" is found reflects an aspect of God's choosing from among believers. At the end of the parable of the laborers (Matthew 20:1-16), God chooses those who live by *grace*;[10] while at the end of the parable of the wedding banquet (Matthew 22:1-14), God chooses those who *lived lives that were fruitful*.[11] The combination of these two traits indicates the extent to which a person will perform when given a task by the Lord.

A similar example can be seen in the training of a young male gymnast. As the routines on the rings began to get complicated and dangerous, more of his available time each day becomes dedicated to gym work, and increased devotion to the sport is required. His coach is always standing within arm's length to break his falls, which are certain to occur. After being caught a number of times, the gymnast learns to trust his coach's ability to save him from harm when he fails. This enables him to perform to a higher level of risk, knowing that his life is safe in the hands of his coach. There is a direct, proportional relationship between high performance and lack of fear . . . and this direct parallels one's life in Christ: We perform better and are more of a risk-taker for the Lord when we are not worried about losing our eternal life. This is what living under free grace is all about.

Jesus is looking for those who are not only loyal and dedicated, but willing to risk all for the sake of knowing and following Him. He is looking for top performers; for a "few good men." Though many are called, it is only those who faithfully walk the path of righteousness that will be chosen.

Those Who are Called (klētos)

In the table below are groups who are "called" (*klētos* - divinely appointed for some work or task) by God in the New Testament. Those who are "chosen", in the expression "many are called (*klētos*), but few are chosen", come from these groups, <u>all of whom are believers</u>. Thus, it cannot be said that those who are called but not chosen are condemned to hell (see Matthew 22:11-14).

All believers are "created in Christ Jesus for good works, which God has appointed for them beforehand" (Ephesians 2:10a), but though they should walk in the works God has pre-planned (Ephesians 2:10b), many believers will fail to do so . . . and will lose the privilege of being chosen for a role/task/position in the age to come.

Verse	Person(s) called	Type of calling
Matthew 20:16	Vineyard laborers	Called into service by the owner of the vineyard
Matthew 22:14	Those (believing Gentiles) other than the originally invited guests (unbelieving Jews)	Invited to join in a festive banquet for the marriage of the king's son
Romans 1:1	Paul	Appointed as an apostle; called to be separated unto the spread of the gospel
Romans 1:6	Believers of the church in Rome	Appointed by Jesus Christ
Romans 1:7	Believers of the church in Rome	Called to holiness

Verse	Person(s) called	Type of calling
Romans 8:28	Believers who love God	Appointed according to His purposes
1 Corinthians 1:1	Paul	Appointed as an apostle
1 Corinthians 1:2	Believers of the church in Corinth	Called to holiness
1 Corinthians 1:24	Believers, both Jews and Greeks	Called to experience the power and wisdom of God in Christ
Jude 1:1	Believers	Called to holiness
Revelation 17:14	Believers	Called to faithfulness (rewarded by being chosen to accompany the Lord when He returns)

3

THE FIRST AND THE LAST

Some have the impression that the next age will find believers in an egalitarian economy: that all believers will be equal in rank and privilege under Christ's rule, all tears will be wiped away[1], all deeds done in the flesh will be forgotten, and everyone will bask in the glory of the Lord. But this view, where accountability for how one lived his life in Christ after becoming saved is overlooked, is simply not supported by Scripture.

A significant portion of the New Testament was written to help the believer mature in his walk with Christ. The epistles were all written to those who had already been saved. The primary intent of the writers was not to tell believers how they could gain eternal life (justification), but how their faithfulness could produce a life of eternal value.[2] In this regard, there are serious warnings in the gospels as well as most of the epistles directed at believers who do not endure in their walk with Christ.

There are many references in the New Testament to being "saved" (*sozo*), but less than half of these mean "eternally saved." The second most common usage of *sozo* means to "*save one's life from becoming useless or ineffectual,*" as in 1 Corinthians 3:15 and 15:2. While one's soul is saved through faith at a point in time, his earthly life is to be saved through the process of sanctification. The believer's justification is always secure, but his earthly life can be wasted, or rendered ineffective, if he rejects the prompting of the Holy Spirit. Scripture indicates that the degree to which a disciple is fully committed to Jesus is the degree to which his life in eternity will be abundant.[3] The thoughts and deeds of every believer in this age affect the quality of his destiny in the next.

In this context, Jesus declares that for many believers "the last shall be first; and first last." This expression is found twice in the gospel of Matthew (19:30 and 20:16), bracketing the parable of the vineyard laborers (20:1-15). Thus the parable is critical to an understanding of Jesus' "first-last, last-first" expression.

First and last in the parable of the vineyard laborers (Matthew 20:1-16)

The parable of the vineyard laborers is part of Jesus' answer to the rich young ruler's question in 19:16 about an abundant eternal inheritance. Seeing that there will be "treasure in heaven" awaiting those who follow Jesus, and realizing he and the other disciples have left all to become disciples, Peter asks (in effect) in 19:27, "What benefit will we receive for being committed disciples?" After assuring Peter of his reward in the age to come, Jesus tells the parable to address the character flaw that Peter's question revealed.

The landowner (or owner of the vineyard) in the parable represents Jesus, and all of the workers represent disciples.[4]

At the beginning of the story a vineyard owner sets out in the morning to hire laborers. It is reasonable to assume that the owner of the vineyard approached all of those he hired with the same proposal: "If you go work in my vineyard, I will pay you *whatever is right.*" Those who were hired first, however, seem to have struck a deal.[5] They would not work without knowing beforehand "how it would benefit them," mirroring the same attitude found in Peter's question. Though the vineyard owner agreed to their terms (a denarius for a day's work), the need for an agreement reflects their lack of faith and trust in the owner to pay them "what is right." Not only would this appear to be somewhat insulting, it placed the owner in the position of being *obligated* to them for their work. While there is nothing unusual about this sort of arrangement in the normal business world where untrustworthy people abound; it takes on an entirely different aspect when the business owner is Jesus. The poor attitude of the contract laborers is further revealed by their envy of fellow workers and their accusation that the owner is being unfair (20:11-12). It is evident they worked only for the wages they demanded, amounting to a *legalistic* working relationship.

The workers hired later in the day readily accepted the owner's proposal to pay them "whatever is right." Their attitude in working could best be described as one of thankfulness to be hired, and a willingness to implicitly trust in the goodness of the landowner . . . amounting to a working relationship based on *grace*. The generosity of the owner recalls the rich young ruler's acknowledgement of Jesus as "*Good* Teacher" in the prior chapter. (See Matthew 19:16.)

In the end, those who worked under grace were bestowed the honor of being paid first, and abundantly,[6] while those who worked legalistically (under a contract) were paid last, and only for the amount they demanded. The sad consequences for the contract laborers were a loss of joy in one's labor, a loss of reward, a loss of honor, a loss of position or privilege, and a proper rebuke by the owner of the vineyard. Note that there was no envy expressed by the "grace" laborers who were hired at the third hour even though they worked eight hours more than those hired at the eleventh hour! Nor did they accuse the landowner of unfairness. The parable indicates that the consequences of each laborer's attitude will be realized at the judgment seat of Christ (at the end of the day when the owner's steward called in the laborers to receive their wages).

Several years before I was a believer, God illustrated this principle in my life. In the summer of 1973, after graduating from Rice University, I took a school-arranged internship with a small architectural firm in Midland, Texas. The owner of the firm was a well-known, published architect whose clients were wealthy oil company executives. There were not many people my age in Midland, so to be constructive with my ample spare time, I took an evening course in lithography at Midland Community College. One day I brought one of my newly-printed lithographs to the office, and pinned it to the wall above my drafting table. That morning, one of our wealthy clients dropped by for a meeting, saw the lithograph, and said, "I'd sure like a copy of that if you have any more left. How much are you selling them for?" Taken by surprise, I told him I had never sold a piece of artwork before, and that I simply gave them to my relatives or friends. He insisted, however, on paying for the drawing and said, "Come up with a price, deliver the drawing to my office, and I'll have my secretary write you a check." He then met with the owner of the firm and left the office an hour later. As soon as he had gone, the two staff architects working with me asked, "Tom, how much are you going to ask for the lithograph?" I told them probably twenty-five dollars. "You are going about this the wrong way," they told me; "These guys have lots of money." After thinking a moment, they both agreed that I should send the drawing over to his office with a note saying, "I couldn't come up with a price. Just pay me what you think it is worth." This sounded like wise advice, though it meant I would have to trust in the generosity of the wealthy client. I sent the drawing with a note to his office and two days later received a check for $200! How foolish I would have been to dictate terms to a man who was so wealthy, and wanted to be generous!

The attempt to put God in our debt, and to live as though He were obligated to meet our demands, is a type of self-righteousness, for it assumes we have earned or merited what God wants to freely give. Self-righteousness living is diametrically opposed to the goal Christ has for our lives . . . for it is putting one's self "first" before everything else.

First and last with the disciples

To hammer home the meaning of the parable of the vineyard laborers, Matthew follows it in 20:20-28 with James' and John's preemptive effort to gain the right to sit at Jesus' side in the coming kingdom. This selfish act greatly displeased the other ten disciples; by which displeasure they appear to be equally guilty . . . due to envy. But Jesus said to them,

> *"You know that the rulers of the Gentiles lord it over them, and those who are great exercise authority over them. Yet it shall not be so among you; but whoever desires to become great among you, let him be your servant.* <u>*And whoever desires to be first among you,*</u> *let him be your slave – just as the Son of Man did not come to be served, but to serve, and to give His life a ransom for many."* (Matthew 20:25-28)

Another aspect of self-righteousness among the disciples is apparent from the parallel passage in Luke 22:24-27. Here we find that the disciples began to argue over which of them should be considered the greatest. Such "fruit-inspecting sessions" contribute to disunity among believers, and destroy fellowship. Jesus confronts this type of relationship a number of times in the gospels. In Luke 18, He describes two men who went up to the temple to pray; one a Pharisee, and the other a tax collector:

> "The Pharisee stood and prayed thus with himself, 'God, I thank You that I am not like other men – extortioners, unjust, adulterers, or even as this tax collector. I fast twice a week; I give tithes of all that I possess.' And the tax collector, standing afar off, would not so much as raise his eyes to heaven, but beat his chest, saying, 'God, be merciful to me a sinner!' I tell you, this man went down to his house justified rather than the other; for everyone who exalts himself will be humbled, and he who humbles himself will be exalted." (Luke 18:10-14)

The Pharisee considered himself "first" and the tax collector "last" before God. But God's ranking of the two was reversed. Jesus does not indicate that the "first" are saved, while the "last" are lost. The use of the word "justified" in 18:14 simply means that the confession of the tax collector was acceptable before God, while the confession of the Pharisee was not.[7] Jesus' ranking suggests an entire range of positions, where first and last are only the extremes. These extremes of behavior are presented so that the believer may be made aware of resulting blessing or harm at the judgment seat of Christ. If the judgment of unfaithful lifestyles is assigned to unbelievers only, a divine "alarm system" is turned off that was designed for believers whose lives may be found drifting toward "destruction".

First and Last in the Millennium

Earlier in the gospel of Luke, Jesus is invited to dinner at the house of one of the rulers of the Pharisees. Upon noticing that those who were invited selected the best seats for themselves, He said,

> "When you are invited by anyone to a wedding feast, do not sit down in the best place, lest one more honorable than you be invited by him; and he who invited you and him

> come and say to you, 'Give place to this man,' and then you begin with shame to take the lowest place. But when you are invited, go and sit down in the lowest place, so that when he who invited you comes he may say to you, 'Friend, go up higher.' Then you will have glory in the presence of those who sit at the table with you. For whoever exalts himself will be humbled, and he who humbles himself will be exalted." (Luke 14:8-11)

Again the issue is not justification (positional righteousness), but "ranking" *within the kingdom*, for the occasion is that of a wedding feast; best understood as an eschatological event.[8] Those who assume their approval before God by their status within the Christian community, observance of religious ritual, position of authority within a church or membership in a specific denomination will find that such criteria have no merit at the judgment seat of Christ. In Philippians 3, Paul considered his own such "pedigree" to be rubbish[9] in contributing to a righteous life in Christ.

So what are the criteria God will use in determining "first" and "last" in the Millennial kingdom? They are the qualities of submissiveness, humility and selflessness (fruits of walking in the Spirit) . . . the opposite criteria of that by which the world operates. The apostle Peter writes: *'Yes, all of you be submissive to one another, and be clothed with humility, for 'God resists the proud, but gives grace to the humble.' Therefore humble yourselves under the mighty hand of God, that He may exalt you in due time, casting all your cares on Him, for He cares for you."* (1Peter 5:5b-6) James says, *"Humble yourselves in the sight of the Lord, and He will lift you up."* (James 4:10) Similarly, the apostle Paul writes, *"Let nothing be done through selfish ambition or conceit, but in lowliness of mind let each esteem others better than himself. Let each of you look out not only for his own interests, but also for the interests of others."* (Philippians 2:3-4) Paul then uses the example of Christ as that for which a believer should model his life, setting forth His humility and selflessness, for which God highly exalted Him. In like manner (with humility and selflessness), believers are to "work out their own salvation with <u>fear and trembling</u>" (Philippians 2:12), for Jesus will someday hold them accountable.

The passage in Luke 14:7-11, where Jesus is invited to dine with a ruler of the Pharisees (mentioned previously), is followed by a parable concerning a great supper given by a man who invited many (14:15-24). Again the allusion is to a Millennial feast, for Jesus responds to the remark *"Blessed is he who shall eat bread in the kingdom of God!"* This echoes the announcement in Revelation 19:9 *"Blessed are those who are called to the marriage supper of the Lamb!"* In both cases, those invited are believers . . . and the unspoken warning is that there are some believers who may not be invited.

In the parable, a number of those invited place their personal needs and desires above those of the man (God) who has invited them, making lame excuses[10] for not accepting. The invitation to this banquet is not an invitation to become justified (saved), but to become a dedicated disciple, as is apparent from the context both before and after the parable. The issue at hand is one of priorities: who comes first in a believer's life, himself or Christ? The shocking realization for those who put Jesus "last" is that they will be *denied access* to the supper;[11] most likely the wedding supper mentioned in Revelation 19:9. Other believers will be "persuaded" to take their places (Luke 14:23).

Summary

This parable, though alluding to a future event, provides a fitting summary to this chapter. Jesus desires that we love Him more than our work and obligations (14:18-19), our family (14:20, 26), our comfort and safety (14:27) and our very lives (14:26). To desire to be a follower of Jesus, we must be willing to pay the cost (14:28) and to forsake all we have (14:33). Only in doing so will we experience all that God desires for us in this life. Failing in this task will bring shame (14:29-30).

Moreover, the work of a disciple should be done in appreciation; not just for the gift of eternal life, but for the opportunity to work for a gracious and loving Master.

Where we place our priorities indicates the importance of Jesus in our lives. Those believers who put Jesus first in this life, He will rank highest in the next age (the reign of Christ during the Millennium). Those believers who put Him last in this life will find they are correspondingly demoted in the next.

The Laborers in the Vineyard
Matthew 20:1-16

Why given: To answer Peter's question in 19:27 "What then will there be for us?"

To whom: To all disciples with regard to their earthly walk in Christ

Topic: Living by law or grace; consequences at the judgment seat of Christ.

Context: Discipleship and sanctification

WORKERS HIRED FIRST (At the beginning of the day)	WORKERS HIRED LATER (At mid-day and afterward)
WORKED FOR PERSONAL GAIN They were unwilling to work unless they had a guaranteed wage.	**WORKED OUT OF A SENSE OF GRATITUDE** They were willing to work regardless of their wage. They were happy to have work to do.
WORKED UNDER A CONTRACT They insisted upon a contract, making the landowner obligated to them.	**WORKED UNDER GRACE** No contract was needed.
DISTRUSTED THE LANDOWNER They thought it possible that the landowner could take advantage of them.	**TRUSTED THE LANDOWNER** The landowner's word was sufficient. They trusted in his character.

WORKERS HIRED FIRST (At the beginning of the day)	WORKERS HIRED LATER (At mid-day and afterward)
HIRED FIRST but PAID LAST A dishonorable end / demotion in rank. "Many are first who shall be last" (Matt. 19:30)	**WERE HIRED LAST but PAID FIRST** An honorable end / preferential treatment. "Many are last who shall be first" (Matt. 19:30)
PAID ACCORDING TO A CONTRACT They received what they deserved under the terms of the contract they negotiated, and nothing more.	**PAID ACCORDING TO GRACE** They were rewarded abundantly and freely, according to the generosity of the landowner. They received far more than they deserved.
UNTHANKFUL TO THE LANDOWNER Accused the landowner of unfairness. No appreciation of grace extended to others. Out of fellowship with the landowner.	**THANKFUL TO THE LANDOWNER** Are as grateful at the end of the day as they were when they were hired. In fellowship with the landowner.
LOSE JOY AND CONTENTMENT Exhibit discontentment and envy of fellow workers. Having a contract provided a basis for comparison with others. Legalism has robbed them of purpose, joy, contentment, and reward.	**EXPERIENCE JOY AND CONTENTMENT** No discontent or envy of fellow workers hired later. No basis for discontent, since work was not done under a contract. All paid at a much higher hourly wage than those who insisted upon a contract.

4

THE GIFT AND THE INHERITANCE

The term "eternal life" in scripture can refer either to its timelessness or its quality ("abundance"). Typically, the timeless aspect is in mind when eternal life is described as a "free gift", as in Romans 5:18 and Ephesians 2:8. This gift (our justification) is given totally and freely, and is, of course, eternal. It cannot be lost. We cannot earn it through good deeds nor can we contribute to it. Jesus' blood purchased our justification, which is appropriated by faith alone. Any attempt to contribute toward one's justification would imply that Jesus' death on the cross was insufficient; and such an attempt would be an insult to God.

"Inherited eternal life" (Matt. 19:29, Luke 18:18), on the other hand, refers to that which is laid up by God as an *inheritance* for a believer in eternity. It refers to the abundant aspect of eternal life rather than its timelessness. Paul says in Ephesians 1:11,

"In Him also we have obtained an inheritance, being predestined according to the purpose of Him who works all things according to the counsel of His will..." Every believer is qualified to partake of this inheritance, for which the Holy Spirit is his downpayment.[1]

Inheritance under Roman law and Mosaic law

In Jesus' day, the concept of inheritance would have been understood from both Jewish and Roman perspectives. Under the Mosaic law, all sons received an equal share of the inheritance, except for the firstborn son, who had the right to a double-share (see Deuteronomy 21:17). Under Roman law, some of an heir's inheritance could be lost under certain circumstances, but there was a foundational portion (*legima portio*) from which a son could never be disinherited. Thus, a portion of his inheritance was guaranteed.

A believer's inheritance can be understood in this same manner: 1) All believers receive a foundational share of the inheritance, and 2) some believers will receive a share much larger than the foundational portion. This distinction is seen in Romans 8:16-17: *"The Spirit Himself bears witness with our spirit that we are children of God, and if children, then heirs – heirs of God and joint heirs with Christ, if indeed we suffer with Him, that we may also be glorified together."* Note the distinction made in verse 17 between "heirs" and "joint heirs". One becomes an heir simply by virtue of being a child of God; but faithfully going through trials is required to become a joint heir with Christ.

The foundational portion

Since the appropriation of the foundational portion of the inheritance by the believer is secured merely by virtue of one's status as a child in the family of God, all believers share equally in this inheritance. This foundational portion would include, but is not limited to, the benefits Christ promised his disciples during the last Passover meal in John 14: an abode in heaven with Christ (14:2-3), a meaningful role in serving by doing the works of God (14:12), answers to prayers (14:13-14), the indwelling Holy Spirit (14:16-17), and inner peace in a hateful world (14:27). Note the illustration of this in the parable of the Prodigal Son in Luke 15:11-32. Despite the rebellious behavior of the younger son, he *did not lose* the welcome to abide in his father's house, his status as a son, his role in the family, and the mercy, forgiveness and love of his father.

The double share

As mentioned earlier, the firstborn son in a Jewish family received a double share of the inheritance. But, unlike the foundational portion, the double share to the firstborn son could be lost. In Genesis 48:5-6, Jacob confers "firstborn" status on Joseph, giving him a double share of the inheritance of the Promised Land through Joseph's two sons, Ephraim and Manasseh.[2] It might be said that this was a reward for the faithfulness of Joseph, and that the biological firstborn son, Reuben, lost his double share due to rebellious behavior (see Genesis 35:22).

With regards to a believer's inheritance, Christ's ranking is that of the firstborn. *"For whom He foreknew, He also predestined to be conformed to the image of His Son, that He might be the* <u>firstborn</u> *among many brethren."* (Romans 8:29) If a believer becomes a "joint heir" with Christ, he then would receive a larger portion of the inheritance. But the status of "joint heir" and the reward of a double portion (in addition to the *legima portio*) is neither automatic nor guaranteed for a believer.

Laying hold of an abundant eternal life

There is an exceedingly-rich inheritance laid up for every believer, which is the *"hope of His calling"* (Ephesians 1:18-19). It is this abundant aspect of eternal life that Paul addresses in 1 Timothy 6:12, where he encourages Timothy to *"lay hold on eternal life"*. The Greek word for "lay hold on" is **epilambanomai**, meaning to "seize upon with one's hands", or "take firm possession of". Timothy was to lay hold of eternal life by "pursuing righteousness" and "fighting the good fight of faith."[3]

The "abundant" aspect of eternal life is in view when an expert in the Law of Moses queries Jesus *"Teacher, what shall I do to <u>inherit</u> eternal life?"* (Luke 10:25) Obviously, the lawyer could not inherit eternal life (justification) from his parents, nor could he appropriate or earn it by following Jesus' recommendation to obey the Mosaic Law. The lawyer's question would be better understood as, *"Teacher, what shall I do to have an inheritance in eternity?"* When Jesus asks him what the answer is from Scripture, the lawyer responds correctly. With regard to the *quality* of eternal life, loving God and one's neighbor have direct application (10:27-28). Jesus' confirmation of this in Luke 10:28 was, *"Do this and you will live."* In other words, "Do this and you will have an <u>abundant life</u> in eternity." The parable of the good Samaritan, which follows in 10:30-37, is given by Jesus to illustrate the direct application of loving one's neighbor to eternal inheritance.[4]

In Mark 10:17-22, Jesus answers the same question for a rich young ruler[5]: *"Good Teacher, what good thing shall I do that I may inherit eternal life?"* From Jesus' response, it appears the young man had already placed his faith in the Lord, for no one can become justified by obedience to the commandments.[6] Further acknowledgment of his faith is indicated by openly kneeling before Jesus and addressing Him as "Good Teacher,"[7] a term that, by Jesus' own admission, would only be appropriate for God. (It should not be discounted that the rich young ruler meant it that way.) The young man's desire was not to become saved (justified),[8] <u>but to be assured of an abundant eternal life matching his wealthy earthly life.</u> Jesus' answer confirms this:

"If you want to be perfect, go, sell what you have and give to the poor, and you will have treasure in heaven; and come, follow Me." (Matthew 19:21)

Jesus knew the young man's heart still clung to earthly riches. What he lacked to be "perfect" (fully-committed, mature in his discipleship) was the ability to separate himself from earthly things. The cure was to sell all of his possessions for the benefit of the poor and follow Jesus. Unfortunately, the man would join a number of Jesus' would-be followers who fell short of faithful discipleship because of their inability to separate themselves from the cares of this world.[9] This is precisely the concern of Jesus when he talks about treasure in heaven in His sermon on the mount:

"No one can serve two masters; for either he will hate the one and love the other, or else he will be loyal to the one and despise the other. You cannot serve God and mammon." (Matthew 6:24)

Such worldly disciples enter the kingdom of heaven but only with great "difficulty" (***dyskolos***) (Matthew 19:23). The apostle Paul says their earthly lives in Christ are saved (preserved), but only "as through fire" (1 Corinthians 3:15). By prioritizing their lives around the acquisition of earthly "treasure," they have neglected the very purpose for which Jesus saved them to begin with, and produced only that which perishes. Their works will be characterized as "wood, hay and stubble," incapable of surviving the Lord's "test by fire" at the bema seat judgment (1 Corinthians 3:12-15). The difficulty of a camel passing through the eye of a needle speaks of the difficulty of a life of great "uncleanness"[10] passing the scrutinizing inspection of the Lord. Such a life would could not appear at the judgment seat of Christ with anything worth commendation were it not for the power and grace of God: *"With men this is impossible, but with God all things are possible."* (Matthew 19:26)

John addresses this same topic in his second epistle. Knowing there will be temptations to stray from loving the Lord (obeying His commandments) and to follow deceivers, he says to his readers: *"Look to yourselves, that you do not lose those things we worked for, but that you may receive a full reward."* (2 John 1:8)

It is also a prominent theme of the epistle to the Hebrews. In Hebrews 1:14-2:4, the author warns that a believer's inheritance ("inherited salvation"[11]) will be diminished if he drifts from the fundamentals of the faith. The consequences of a disobedient life are justly deserved, and are inescapable.

Inheritance in the Millennial Kingdom

Much of a believer's inheritance will be realized in the coming Messianic Kingdom, a literal kingdom where Christ will rule on the earth. (See Chapter 2.) Paul warns the Ephesians that their inheritance in Christ's kingdom can be *forfeited* (Ephesians 5:1-6) by failing to follow the will of the Lord in their process of sanctification. He repeats this warning in Galatians 5:17-21,[12] and has the same thought in mind in Titus 3:7-8, where those who have believed are warned to be careful to maintain good works. Paul further adds in Romans 8:17 that we are *"joint heirs with Christ, <u>if indeed we suffer with Him</u>"*; indicating that "laying hold" of one's full inheritance is connected with enduring as a believer. The word "suffer" (***sympascho***) speaks of a willingness to experience the same trials and persecutions that Christ did, for the sake of righteousness.[13] If a believer shrinks back in his faith when trials and persecutions arise,[14] his inheritance in Jesus' earthly kingdom will be affected.

In the parable of the unjust steward (Luke 16:1-12) Jesus emphasizes the need to invest one's time wisely in this life so that one may have an *abundant* entrance into the next. Jesus notes that unjust (presumably unsaved) people pay more attention to laying up for their "golden years" on earth (an inheritance that will deteriorate) than righteous people do to lay up an inheritance that can never fade away! Those believers who are faithful in this task will be entrusted with more, but those who have been unfaithful in this life will not only have lost the trust of God, they will be in danger of losing even what was "their own" (16:12)![15] The same danger is echoed in Colossians 2:18-19, where Paul admonishes, *"Let no one cheat you of your reward;"* which may be lost by not holding fast to Christ. Instead, Paul says, *". . . whatever you do, do it heartily, as to the Lord and not to men, knowing that from the Lord you will receive* the reward of the inheritance; *for you serve the Lord Christ. But he who does wrong will be repaid for what he has done, and there is no partiality."* (Colossians 3:23-25)

Paul's warning derives from the words of Jesus in the parable of the talents (Matthew 25:14-30). Of the three believers, the last does nothing with the goods to which he was entrusted. He is judged to be lazy and wicked by his lord, who says, *". . . take the talent from him, and give it to him who has ten talents. For to everyone who has, more will be given, and he will have abundance;* but from him who does not have, even what he has will be taken away.*"* What the wicked servant "did not have" was a profit earned from his lord's goods. What "he has" that was taken away were the goods (the opportunities, the blessings, the responsibilities) entrusted to him, which correspond to one's *inheritance* (opportunities, blessings, responsibilities) in Jesus' administration of His kingdom (Jesus' rule during the Millennium).

As mentioned before, there is a tendency to attribute the negative aspects of this parable to unbelievers; but even a casual look at the context and wording refutes this idea: a) The three servants are the "the lord's own servants;" b) they are judged for their handling of their lord's goods, not their opportunity to believe; c) the faithful servants are rewarded with joy and added responsibility, not justification; d) the unfaithful servant is berated for his laziness and wickedness, not his unbelief; e) the unfaithful servant loses the joy of his lord and the goods entrusted to him, not eternal life; and f) the unfaithful servant is cast into the "outer court" where it is dark,[16] not out of Christ's kingdom.

In Ephesians 4 and 5, Paul exhorts believers to walk "worthy of their calling" in Christ, to be imitators of God, not grieving the Holy Spirit. Paul knows full well a believer can do just the opposite. He contrasts the faithful walk of a believer with a worldly, carnal walk of a believer; one that he would expect to find only in a Gentile. Paul warns in 5:3-6 that a believer who has a lifestyle of sexual immorality, uncleanness, and idolatry <u>will not have an inheritance</u> in the kingdom of Christ and God!

In Galatians 5:17-21 Paul again addresses the problem of works of the flesh and says, "*. . . those who practice such things will <u>not inherit</u> the kingdom of God.*" A few verses later, in 6:7-8, he adds, "*Do not be deceived, God is not mocked; for whatever a man sows, that will he also reap. For he who sows to the flesh will of the flesh reap corruption, but he who sows to the Spirit will of the Spirit reap <u>everlasting life</u>.*" Here is another reference to the *quality* of everlasting life, in essence meaning "life of everlasting abundance." The emphasis is on the abundant quality of eternal life (particularly in the coming kingdom), not the timelessness of it, for one cannot be justified by his works (sowing to the Spirit). Moreover the preventive measure Paul gives to avoid corruption[17] is not to believe in Christ, but to endure (not grow weary, not lose heart) in one's walk.

Lost inheritance cannot be recovered

A number of times, while growing up, I have been reminded (by my parents or others) that "You've got but one life to live: make the most of it." Though sayings of this sort are usually uttered with a worldly view in mind, they have a Christian application.

A believer can only contribute to his eternal inheritance in this life. There is no indication in Scripture that we can contribute to it afterward. Opportunity lost here is probably lost for eternity. We should not take our status as sons of God lightly, nor assume that our justification alone guarantees us an abundant future with Christ.

Jesus' tale of the two sons in Luke 15:11-32 reveals that the younger son lost his inheritance through riotous living (15:13, 31). The joyful reunion with his father was made possible by his repentance and return to his father, *but the lost portion of his inheritance was not restored.*

Similarly, the writer of Hebrews puts forth the example of Esau, who sold his birthright for a bowl of soup. Esau valued worldly things more than spiritual things, a character flaw that undoubtedly led to God's selection of his younger brother to continue the lineage to Christ. Note carefully how the writer of Hebrews applies Esau's lack of priorities to a believer's walk: *"For you know that afterward, when he* [Esau] *wanted to inherit the blessing, he was rejected, for he found no place for repentance, though he sought it diligently with tears."* (Hebrews 12:17) The "blessing" that Esau lost was his prominent future role in the family. Just as with Esau, many Christians may have their inheritance diminished by taking God's grace for granted; and also just as with Esau, they may find that repentance comes too late to alter the consequences.

This is precisely the meaning of Jesus' parable of the rich man in Luke 12:16-20. The parable follows a discourse on discipleship (see 12:4-12) and precedes concern over where the believer's heart is directed (12:31-34) and the importance of being faithful servants (12:35-40). The rich man in the parable is a "fool" because the Son of Man came at an hour he did not expect. He was found totally unprepared, having only laid up treasure for himself on earth. Once his life was "required of him," there was no longer any place for repentance.[18]

Summary

God has laid up a rich inheritance for all believers; but a portion of this inheritance is "laid up in a trust" to be given as a reward for a faithful, obedient, and selfless life.[19] It would be foolish to think that one's eternal inheritance is unaffected by carnal living; and un-biblical to equate one's inheritance with the gift of eternal life (justification). Knowing that the quality of his eternal life is at stake, how then should we live? The apostle Peter answers this question for us: *"Therefore, brethren, be even more diligent to make your call and election sure, for if you do these things you will never stumble; for so an entrance will be supplied to you abundantly into the everlasting kingdom of our Lord and Savior Jesus Christ."* (1 Peter 1:10-11)

Biblical Examples of Losing Inheritance

Person(s)	Inheritance Lost	Reason	Verses
Esau	Double share of inheritance as first born; father's blessing	Fornication; profaneness; worldliness	Genesis 25:29-34 Hebrews 12:14-17
Reuben	Double share of inheritance as first born; Given to Joseph instead (in Manasseh & Ephraim)	Disobedience; rebellion (laying with his father's concubine)	Genesis 35:22, 48:3-6
Entire generation of Children of Israel	Inheritance of Promised Land	Lack of faith	Numbers 13:1-4, 14:20-23
Prodigal Son	His share of the inheritance	Rebellion; worldliness	Luke 15:11-32
Rich young ruler	Eternal inheritance	Clinging to worldly wealth	Mark 10:17-22, Matthew 19:16-22
Carnal believer	Eternal inheritance	Immorality; uncleanness; idolatry	Ephesians 5:3-6
Shallow believer	Eternal inheritance	Does not endure suffering	Romans 8:17
Disobedient believer	Eternal inheritance	Please men rather than God	Colossians 3:22-25
Lazy believer	Eternal inheritance	Laziness; poor stewardship	Matthew 25:14-30
Tribe of Ephraim (?)	Inheritance in Millennium	Idolatry; rebellion	Hosea 7:13-16; Missing tribe in Revelation 7:4-8

5

ROBES AND WEDDING GARMENTS

A believer is clothed with the righteousness of Christ at the point of his justification. This "robe of righteousness" is not made by the believer, but is provided graciously by God. It is a free gift, purchased with the precious blood of Christ. But there is another type of clothing that every believer should have when he appears before the Savior at the judgment seat of Christ. It is his wedding garment. This garment is not freely given; it is purchased and adorned by the believer. It is the product of a life lived obediently to the will of God; one that produces good works.

A believer's robe of righteousness

Ever since Adam's sin in the Garden of Eden, man has had to be clothed (Genesis 3:21). Scripture teaches that man needs a spiritual "covering" for his sin nature to be able to have a relationship with God. In the Old Testament, this righteous standing before God was attained by grace through faith. This is seen in Genesis 15:6 (enlarged upon by Paul in Romans 4:1-8), in the faith of Abraham. An individual's covering for sin in the Old Testament is metaphorically described as a "robe of righteousness" (Job 29:14, Isaiah 61:10). As New Testament believers, our "robe of righteousness" is Christ himself[1] (Galatians 3:27). Thus when God sees us from a positional standpoint, he sees Christ.

The robe of righteousness is a functional garment, not necessarily a radiant one, for it represents our justification, our status as children in the family of God, and our identity with Christ. In this sense, this robe is the "standard-issue uniform" for every believer. No one believer's robe of righteousness is more ornate or beautiful than the robe of any other believer. It dictates no rank or privilege, for in Christ all are one, both Jew and Greek, slave and free, male and female. Since its benefits are appropriated at the point of justification, the robe of righteousness (unlike the believer's wedding garment) has little eschatological significance.

While the robe of righteousness is the same for all believers, it is also the *minimum* clothing for all believers. It is a foundational undergarment, not a tuxedo. Its function is for *identity*, not for representing faithfulness or endurance under persecution.

The wedding garment in Jewish culture

In contrast to the robe of righteousness, the believer's wedding garment is neither "standard" nor "issued," and its purpose is entirely eschatological. The concept of a "garment" as representative of a *faithful lifestyle* can be seen in an orthodox Jewish wedding. In Jesus' day, a Jewish groom would travel to his prospective bride's house, purchase his betrothed at a considerable cost, give her gifts intended to help her remember him, and return to his own home to prepare a place for her. At this point, the two were legally "husband and wife". During the groom's absence, the betrothed was not only to remain sanctified, she was to prepare herself for her future life together with her husband. So serious was this relationship that unfaithfulness on the part of the bride during this period of time could result in her death by stoning . . . the precise reason that Joseph wanted to divorce Mary quietly when she was found to be with child (Matthew 1:19). The bride would typically have a full year or more to prepare for the consummation of her marriage. Much of her time was invested in making ready her trousseau so that she would be radiantly beautiful at the appearing of her groom.

Being that the groom had not only purchased her at a great cost, given her expensive gifts, and had spent the last year preparing a place for her, it would be hard to imagine the scene where he appears unexpectedly (usually at midnight) to find that his bride had done little-to-nothing in the year since he purchased her . . . without a wedding dress, make-up, jewelry or perfume, and unprepared for her role as a wife and a future mother. Such laziness and lack of gratefulness would be almost unthinkable! The resulting loss of joy, trust, and intimacy with her groom would mar the wedding celebration, as well as her married life to come.[2]

The wedding garment in eschatology

The eschatological significance of a "wedding garment" is illustrated in the parable of the wedding banquet in Matthew 22:1-14. After his invitation to the wedding banquet for his son is refused by those who were originally invited (the nation of Israel), the king sends his servant out into the streets to invite all they can find, both "good" and "bad." The "good" and the "bad" represent believers who come to faith in Christ with varying moral backgrounds. Some are morally good and devout, while others are despised in the Jewish culture of that day, like the tax collectors and harlots mentioned by Jesus in the previous chapter.[3] The allusion here is to a wedding banquet within the kingdom of heaven, most certainly understood by Jews to be a millennial event on earth, not a heavenly event.

Prior to the seating of the guests for the banquet, the king enters the hall to take notice of those who have accepted his invitation. To his displeasure, the king finds a man not properly attired for the occasion: he is not wearing a "wedding garment." Herein is a seeming theological dilemma. The man has accepted the king's invitation (symbolic of justification), yet he is obviously out of favor with the king. After being addressed as "friend," he is graciously given the opportunity to defend his lack of proper attire. But he is speechless: a sign that he had no excuse; or at least none that would satisfy the king. The king then unceremoniously has the unwelcome guest bound hand and foot, and casts[4] him outside into the night,[5] where there is great remorse.[6]

The only other passage in the New Testament mentioning both a wedding garment and a wedding banquet is Revelation 19:7-9. Here the fine linen garment of the bride (who has "made herself ready") represents her *righteous works* (***dikaioma***[7]). It would therefore appear that the man without a wedding garment in the Matthew passage was a believer who was unprepared for his union with Christ, similar to the betrothed mentioned previously. He had wasted his "betrothal period" and was found with no righteous works. The king's anger is evident in that he binds the man hand and foot, preventing his re-entry into the place of joy and feasting. He was not counted worthy to attend a banquet with Abraham, Isaac and Jacob (see Matthew 8:11-12) and others who were faithful in their walk. Though "darkness" can sometimes indicate eternal punishment, this is clearly not the case in this parable.[8]

The distinction between robes of "positional righteousness" and robes of "righteous deeds" is also made in 2 Corinthians 5:2-4, where Paul says

"For in this [tent] *we groan, earnestly desiring to be clothed with our habitation which is from heaven, if indeed, having been clothed, we shall not be found naked. For we who are in this tent groan, being burdened, not because we want to be unclothed, but further clothed, that mortality may be swallowed up in life."*

How can a believer, being clothed with the righteousness of Christ, show up "naked" (or improperly dressed[9]) at the judgment seat of Christ? He can show up improperly dressed (without a wedding garment) if he does not mature in his walk with Christ, if he continually grieves the Holy Spirit, and if he obstinately refuses to follow the will of God.

The making of the wedding garment

As a believer, one is to be dressed with more than simply his "robe of righteousness." But in order to begin preparation of a wedding garment, a believer must first put off the "old man." Paul introduces this necessity in Romans 13:14 where he admonishes his readers to *"make no provision for the flesh."* Paul continued this idea in Philippians 3:3-9, where he put away his confidence in his fleshly "garment," desiring rather to be found "in Christ." He saw his former Hebrew pedigree as dung[10] (***skybalon***), indicating that it was *worse* than useless. In fact, Paul suggests that placing confidence in the flesh as a replacement for "being conformed to Jesus' death" would be *offensive* to God. Another illustration of putting off the "old man" is given to us in Mark 10:50, where Bartimaeus, having miraculously received his sight, casts aside his old garment to follow Jesus.[11]

Of what, then, is a believer's wedding garment to be made? In Matthew 13:45-46 an extremely valuable pearl (the Church) is found by a merchantman (Christ), who sells all that he owns (giving His very life) to purchase it. A pearl is an impurity covered by concentric layers of calcium carbonate, resulting in a radiantly beautiful and valuable object.[12] The impurity inside the pearl is hidden by the beauty of the pearl's covering. While it may take merely a few layers to hide the impurity, the real beauty of a valuable pearl comes from repeatedly-added thin iridescent layers that give it a depth and radiance not found in other pearls . . . a picture of the sanctification process. It might be noted from this parable that the merchant (Jesus) saw great worth in the pearl (all those who believe) before he even bought it! *". . . while we were yet sinners, Christ died for us"!* (Rom. 5:8) Likewise, the Jewish groom saw great beauty or worth in his bride-to-be long before she had prepared her trousseau or adorned herself to meet him.

The making of one's wedding garment emphasizes the more personal, intimate aspects of our love for Christ. Referring again to the Jewish betrothal period, the bride's love for her groom would be displayed by the amount of time, effort and resources she devoted to the preparation for her wedding. Such effort would include her personal preparation for the duties and responsibilities of married life, the making of her trousseau for the wedding, maintaining her personal health and beauty, and separation from any activity that would diminish the joy of the relationship. This effort would be visible to those around her, and as such, would bring increasing glory to her betrothed as the day of his appearing approached. It also would display the extent of her faith and trust in his promises to her; not yet realized, but expected. In this sense, her wedding garment is an outward, visible expression of her faith, hope, and love for her betrothed. *In short, the wedding garment is the manifestation of the works of the believer.* It is to be a clean, radiant and dazzling garment:

> *"Let us be glad and rejoice and give Him glory, for the marriage of the Lamb has come, and His wife has made herself ready." And to her it was granted to be arrayed in fine*

linen, clean and bright, **for the fine linen is the righteous acts of the saints**. *(Rev. 19:7-8)*

In a believer's process of sanctification, he is to put on an outer garment consisting of the "new man," of tender mercies, kindness, humility, meekness, longsuffering, and love (Colossians 3:10-14, 1 Peter 5:5); to gird himself with selflessness (John 13:4, 14); to put on the power and armor of God (Ephesians 6:10-11) and to adorn himself with good works (1 Timothy 2:10). The underlying meaning of Matthew 6:28-30 is that one should seek God's righteousness (pursue righteous acts[13]), being assured that in doing so he will find himself clothed by God in splendor surpassing that of Solomon!

The dangers of ill-preparedness

The preparation of the wedding garment is not automatic, easy or inexpensive. Hard work is required, even with the assistance of the Holy Spirit, to subdue the flesh and put off the "old man." Stubbornness and pride have caused many Christians to set aside the task at hand. If a believer continually grieves the Holy Spirit and hardens his heart to the will of God, he will end up in a similar state to that of the Laodicean church, described in Revelation 3:17-18:

> "Because you say, 'I am rich, have become wealthy, and have Need of nothing' – and do not know that you are wretched, miserable, poor, blind, and naked – I counsel you to buy from Me gold refined in the fire, that you may be rich; and white garments, that you may be clothed, that the shame of your nakedness may not be revealed . . ."

There are two important facets to this passage regarding clothing: 1) the gold adornment and white garments were to be purchased from God; they are not part of the free gift of eternal life. As such, these garments do not represent positional righteousness, but the costly effort it takes to endure as a follower of Christ, producing good works. Without this endurance one will stand shamefully "ill-dressed" someday before the Lord. 2) "White" (*leukos*) garments are those that are "dazzling," "brilliant" or "radiant," representing the sort of clothing we would normally wear only for special occasions, to a formal affair, or in this case, to a wedding. In the age to come, our "wedding garment" will be a sign of our faithfulness to Christ, and of our level of service to Him.

It is quite possible that the Laodicean church represents those who come to faith in Jesus during the tribulation period. If so, they are warned about their works not only in Revelation 3, but in Revelation 16:15, where Jesus says, *"Behold, I am coming as a thief. Blessed is he who watches, and keeps his garments, lest he walk naked and they see his shame."* The emphasis is clearly on the believer's works, and his appearance before men. He is to "keep" (*tereo*), or guard / protect / maintain his outer garment, so that it will be unspotted[14] from walking in the world. Jesus said, *"Let your light so shine before men, that they may see your good works and glorify your Father in heaven."*[15] A believer's "shining" or "radiance" before men is his works, which he is continually to maintain to bring glory to God. Without these works, one's faith is not evident, and is not "justified" before men (James 2:24). Such a faith is inert, or dead (James 2:26), as is illustrated by the "nakedness" of the believer.

Insight from Revelation 3:4-5

While it is evident that a believer's radiant outer garment represents his righteous works, Revelation 3:4-5 contains a problematic statement that must be dealt with. The church in Sardis is the "dead church" (Revelation 3:1) among the seven churches in Revelation chapters two and three. This church is characterized by its lack of good works:

"... you have a name that you are alive, but you are dead. Be watchful, and strengthen the things which remain, that are ready to die, for I have not found your works perfect before God." (3:1b-2)

"You have a few names even in Sardis who have not defiled their garments; and they shall walk with Me in white, for they are worthy. He who overcomes shall be clothed in white garments, and I will not blot out his name from the Book of Life; but I will confess his name before My Father and before His angels." (3:4-5)

The white (radiant) garments are promised to those believers who are "worthy." They will be commended to God at the judgment seat of Christ. However, the statement "I will not blot out his name from the Book of Life" has been used by some to support the false idea that failure to be counted as a "worthy" believer could result in loss of justification.

To understand this apparent dilemma, it must be remembered that Sardis was part of the Roman Empire, and as such, was subject to Roman law. There were levels of legal and social privileges available to those who lived in the Empire, and most of these were available only to Roman *citizens*. A citizen of Rome had the right to vote, the right to hold office, the right to a trial (if arrested), the right to wear the Roman toga, and the right to become a soldier in the Roman army. The apostle Paul, for example, could not be interrogated under scourging since he was a Roman citizen.[16] It would therefore have been important for a governor to keep an updated list of the citizens within his jurisdiction.

The privileges of citizenship could be lost, however, by failing to abide by a number of laws and ethical standards. To retain these privileges, one could not amass great debt, commit serious crimes (like murder, treason, and theft), engage in immoral behavior, cheat in his business dealings or commit treason. Failure to abide by such laws could result in a revoking of citizenship privileges . . . and once lost they could not be regained. Treason was the worst possible crime under Roman law, for it displayed a total lack of respect and gratitude for the privileges of being a citizen, which were freely granted for those born of Roman citizens, and was a rejection of all that Rome stood for. Moreover, such a person would be shamed, and thought a fool by those who longed for such privileges, and who, due to conditions of birth or lack of wealth, were denied the opportunity to become citizens.

Dr. David Anderson, president of Grace School of Theology, explains,

> ". . . only half the residents of Rome were citizens. When a citizen committed an unusually barbarous crime, the city officials ceremoniously erased his name from the book of citizens. He remained as a resident, but lost the rights and privileges of a citizen. Hence, the possibility of having one's name taken from the book of life would not threaten one's residence in the kingdom, but it would threaten his rewards in the kingdom."[17]

This is the likely intent of Jesus' comment that He would not "blot out" the names of those who are written in the Book of Life.[18] Supporting this intent is the fact that the "blotting out" of Revelation 3:5 is juxtaposed against the preferable (and opposite) possibility: that Jesus will confess the believer's name before His Father. It is likely, therefore that "blotting out" is equivalent to being "denied" before the Father at the judgment seat of Christ (see Matthew 10:33).[19]

Paralleling the rewards for faithful believers at the judgment seat of Christ, a Roman citizen was entitled to the best seats in amphitheaters (to attend a banquet with Abraham, Isaac and Jacob – Matthew 8:11), entitled to wear the Roman toga (to wear a radiant garment – Revelation 3:4), entitled to fight in the Roman army (to fight alongside the Lamb - see Revelation 17:14), and to hold political office (to rule with Christ – 2 Timothy 2:12). All of these direct correlations to Roman citizenship would not have been missed by the believers in the church at Sardis. Similarly, Paul declared to the Philippians that they had a heavenly citizenship (far better than Roman citizenship!), and therefore should walk following his example, and stand fast in the Lord. (Philippians 3:17-4:1)

Summary

Just as Jesus once searched for a "pearl of great price", He is today searching for "pearls of great price" (individual believers), whose radiance will speak of their abiding love for Him, and their preparedness to serve in the Millennial kingdom. We are called to appear before Him with more than simply our "robes of righteousness." Yet many Christians, by the worldly, carnal lifestyle they are living, are destined to face Jesus will only the bare essential "garments" at the imminent appearing of their Savior. They will likely face a disappointed Groom.[20]

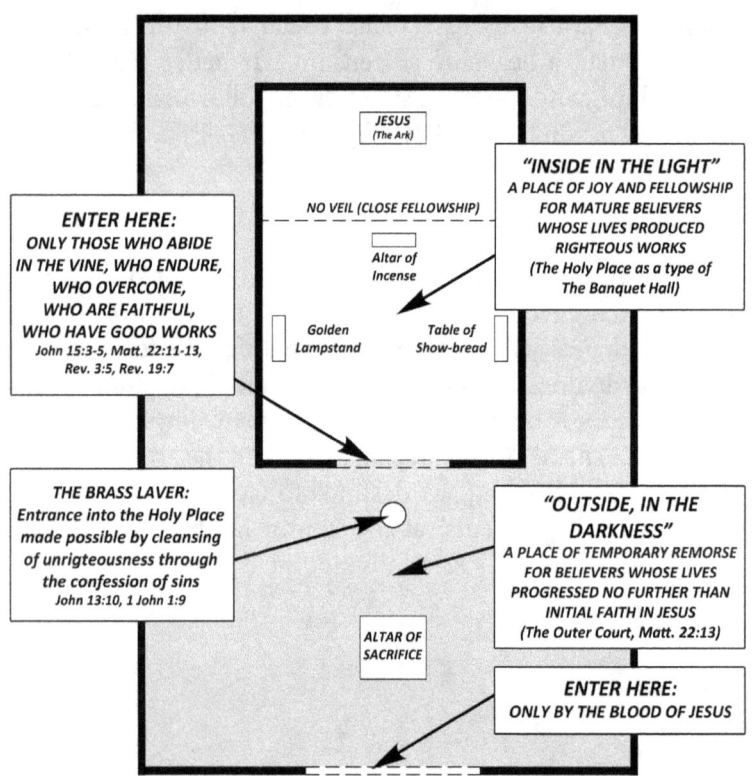

THE TABERNACLE/TEMPLE AS A TYPE OF THE WEDDING BANQUET SITE OF MATT. 22:1-14

6

CONFESSING AND DENYING

My wife and I are friends with a married couple who claim to be big fans of University of Oklahoma football. They both have degrees from OU, but that fact alone does not make them big fans. They fly or drive to every Oklahoma football game (for which they have season tickets), often spending an entire weekend away from home. They wear OU clothing continually during football season. Their cars display OU stickers and have license plate holders. Their house is decorated with OU paraphernalia along with a flag prominently displayed in their front yard; and they love to talk about their team whenever the opportunity presents itself in public. Whether the football team is having a winning season or not makes no difference to their routine or enthusiasm. I suspect that they have donated a considerable sum to the University of Oklahoma over the years. No one could accuse them of being shy or lacking in their support.

Jesus desires that our discipleship be very much like this. We should ask ourselves, having already been "graduated" into the kingdom, if our lifestyle expresses devotion to God. Another way this has been asked is, "If Christianity was against the law; would there be enough evidence to convict you of the crime?"

The Bible terms used for this sort of devotion/discipleship (or lack of it) are "confessing" and "denying." A familiar passage on "confessing" is Romans 10:9-10, "... *if you* confess *with your mouth the Lord Jesus and* believe *in your heart that God has raised Him from the dead, you will be saved. For with the heart one* believes *unto righteousness, and with the mouth* confession *is made unto salvation.*" Two aspects of a believer's life are depicted here: 1) *Believing unto righteousness* (justification) and 2) *confessing unto salvation* (saved from the power of sin; sanctification). Confession (***homologeō*** – "to say the same") is the outward act of a believer in proclaiming Christ in his life, both in words and actions, to everyone around him. It is the opposite of "denying" Christ, which a believer can do by living a carnal, worldly and selfish life. He can also "deny" by being silent to avoid ridicule or outright persecution. Though he has eternal life, one would not think it, for there appears little difference between his lifestyle and that of an unbeliever.

Confessing/denying and discipleship

The tenth chapter of the gospel of Matthew contains Jesus' exhortation to his apostles about discipleship: what they were to do, how they should travel, what they should expect, and how they should react to rejection and persecution. In the last half of the chapter, Jesus talks about what it takes to be a worthy disciple. In 10:32-33 Jesus declares, "*... whoever* confesses *Me before men, him will I also* confess *before My Father who is in heaven. But whoever* denies *Me before men, him will I also* deny *before My Father who is in heaven.*" A "confessing" disciple is one who is willing to be demeaned for the sake of his Savior

Confessing And Denying

(10:26), is unafraid to openly speak the word of God (10:27), and is one who is willing to suffer persecution and death for his faith (10:28). He is one who loves Jesus more than his family (10:37), his own aspirations (10:38), and even his own life (10:39). Jesus will likewise "confess" (commend) this disciple before His Father in heaven.

As can be seen from the context of Matthew 10, "confessing" does *not* mean believing unto justification (gaining eternal life). It is a term that applies strictly to a believer's walk with Christ *after* he is justified. For instance, Paul commends Timothy for his "good <u>confession</u>" before men, comparing it to Jesus' "good <u>confession</u>" (His faithfulness unto death) before Pontius Pilate in 1 Timothy 6:12-13. The writer of Hebrews similarly exhorts his readers to "hold fast to the <u>confession</u> of our hope without wavering" (Hebrews 10:23).

"Denying" Christ is also descriptive of discipleship. A believer denies Christ by doing things that are the opposite of "confessing": failing to proclaim the word of God among men; shrinking back in his faith due to persecution; choosing the admiration of his family over the admiration of Jesus; placing his own life goals above following Jesus; and loving himself more than Jesus. Jesus will testify of this believer before His Father; causing the believer to be <u>denied</u> the privileges in eternal life accorded to those disciples who were faithful.

There are several illustrations of "denying" by disciples in the gospel of John. Nicodemus comes to Jesus *by night* possibly due to fear of being associated with Jesus by the Sanhedrin (John 3:1-2). Similarly, the parents of the blind man whom Jesus healed refuse to confess Christ for fear of being put out of the synagogue (John 9:18-23). In 12:42, John states that many rulers of the Jews did not confess Jesus for the same fear . . . indicating that their love for their position and prominence outweighed their love for the Lord.

In selecting his twelve disciples, it is likely that Jesus sought those who would be unashamed to be in His presence; who would continue to follow Him during his years of ministry even when losing the support of their friends, family, or the religious authorities.

Confessing/denying and the judgment seat of Christ

In 2 Timothy 2:3-10 Paul emphasizes to Timothy the need to "endure hardship as a good soldier of Jesus Christ," and to be hard-working in the face of persecution. In 2:15, he exhorts Timothy to *"Be diligent to present yourself* approved to God, *a worker who does not need to be ashamed, rightly dividing the word of truth."* "Approved" (***dokimos***) means "acceptable," though perhaps a more specific meaning of "passing the test of integrity"[1] would have been understood by those living in Paul's day. Sandwiched between these admonitions to excel, Paul inserts a saying addressed to believers that is frequently misinterpreted; primarily by those who hold that a believer can lose eternal life. The correct interpretation, however, proves just the opposite:

> [11] *This is a faithful saying:*
>   *For if we died with Him, we shall also live with Him.*
> [12] *If we* endure, *we shall also reign with Him.*
>   *If we* deny *Him, He will also deny us.*
> [13] *If we do not believe*[2]*, He remains faithful;*
>   *He cannot deny Himself.* (2 Timothy 2:11-13)

In these three verses Paul covers the foundational truths of justification, faithful discipleship, and eternal security. *If we died with Him* (identified with Him in His death on the cross) *we shall live with Him* (have eternal life). *If we endure* (are faithful in our discipleship), *we shall also reign with Him* (a reward for faithfulness). *If we deny Him* (continually live as though we did not know Him), *He will also deny us* (treat us in the same manner before the Father). *If we stop believing*[2] (abandon the faith after having received eternal life), *He remains faithful* (to His promise of eternal life); *He cannot deny Himself* (He cannot break His promise).

The privilege of reigning with Christ, and more, is denied for those believers who do not endure. Paul follows the above passage with the explanation that, *"... in a great house there are not only vessels of gold and silver, but also of wood and clay, some for honor and some for dishonor. Therefore, if anyone cleanses himself from the latter, he will be a vessel for honor, sanctified and useful for the Master, prepared for every good work."* (2 Timothy 2:20-21)

Few Christians realize that perhaps the greatest obstacle to the growth of God's kingdom does not come from unbelievers, but *believers who lead worldly lives!* By their poor witness, they actually work against the purposes of God. Paul had this in mind in Philippians 3:18-19, *"For many walk, of whom I have told you often, and now tell you even weeping, that they are* <u>enemies</u> *of the cross of Christ: whose end is destruction, whose god is their belly, and whose glory is their shame – who set their mind on earthly things."* That is, their lifestyles are directly opposed to the cross of Christ. They will face "destruction" at the judgment seat of Christ,[3] for their god is their stomach, and their glory is something to be ashamed of. They have pursued earthly things, not righteousness.

This "destruction" (Philippians 3:19) at the judgment seat of Christ is not condemnation to hell. Rather it is destruction of all that one's carnal, faithless lifestyle has "built" in this life. In 1 Corinthians 3:9-17 Paul says we, as believers, are God's building (***oikomdomē***); more aptly put, His "construction project." With His help we are to build upon the foundation which is Christ (his death for our sins). In this sense we are metaphorically constructing and adorning a building through the lives we lead. The goal of every believer should be to build with materials that endure unto eternity. If we use defiled, corrupted, rotting materials, our "building" will not only be unattractive; it will be structurally unstable. In the real world of construction, such a building would not pass inspection by city officials, and would not be certified for human occupancy. To the degree of its "rottenness," the building would be torn down, perhaps all the way to the foundation. All of the planning, labor and materials invested would be destroyed (1 Corinthians 3:17), leaving little in the way of a suitable habitation.

Furthermore, we are not constructing just any building by the way we live, but *God's temple* (1 Corinthians 3:16), a building that is designed for praise and worship; one that is beautiful outside and in; one which proclaims the God who dwells within; one that is a beacon to others; and one that will endure the test of time: "*. . . and the rain descended, the floods came, and the winds blew and beat on that house; and it did not fall, for it was founded on the rock.*" [4] Regardless of the way in which a believer builds, his foundation *will not fail,* for the "rock" of Jesus is a sure foundation.

Confessing/denying, and eternal security

The faithfulness of Jesus to his promise of eternal life (as mentioned previously from 2 Timothy 2:13) applies not only to a believer who has lived a "denying lifestyle," but to those who have temporarily fallen out of fellowship with God. Under fear for his life, Peter denied the Lord three times, despite being forewarned of this by Jesus Himself only hours previous:

> *"Then He said, 'I tell you, Peter, the rooster shall not crow this day before you will deny three times that you know Me.'"* (Luke 22:34)

The English translation of "deny" in this verse does not convey the full force of the Greek word ***aparneomai***, which means to *utterly, completely deny,* or to *disown.*[5] Despite his "utter denial," Peter did not lose his justification, because it was not his responsibility for safe-keeping to begin with.[6] It is Jesus who keeps us eternally secure, continually interceding for us before the Father.[7] In the same conversation with Peter, Jesus tells him:

> *"Simon, Simon! Indeed, Satan has asked for you, that he may sift you as wheat. But I have prayed for you, that your faith should not fail; and when you have returned to Me, strengthen your brethren."* (Luke 22:31-32)

At no point was Peter's justification in jeopardy, despite his complete denial of the Lord. Through brokenness and repentance,[8] he did indeed return to Jesus, and was later martyred for his faith. Peter's denial is a good illustration that all words spoken against the Lord by men are forgivable. Jesus said, *"Anyone who speaks a word against the Son of Man, it will be forgiven him . . ."* (Matthew 12:32).

The most alarming passage relating to a believer's "denying lifestyle" is found in Hebrews 10:26-27, where such a lifestyle is one of willful sin.[9] For these believers, there no longer remains a "sacrifice for sins" (10:26); that is, they are subject to severe disciplinary action . . . to the fearful and indignant reaction of our Savior. It is by the blood of Jesus that we can enter the "Holy of Holies" and live a life acceptable unto God (10:19). The author's concern is *loss of fellowship*, not loss of justification. The apostle John words it this way:

> *"If we say that we have <u>fellowship</u> with Him, and walk in darkness, we lie and do not practice the truth. But if we walk in the light as He is in the light, we have fellowship with one another, and the blood of Jesus Christ His Son cleanses us from all sin."* (1 John 1:6-7)

Believers with willfully-sinning lifestyles work against the cause of Christ, and are described as "adversaries" (***hypenantios***), meaning "contrary ones." Their worthless works will be devoured by the fiery indignation of the Lord at the judgment seat of Christ (1 Corinthians 3:12-15). This fearful possibility is rarely mentioned in the pulpits of America's churches. As a result, many believers return home from church each Sunday under little conviction in the following week to mature in their faith or to depart from lifestyles that "deny" the grace by which they were saved.

Summary

"Confessing" and "denying" are portrayed in Scripture as contrasting lifestyles of *believers*, those who have already been granted eternal life. A believer guilty of exhibiting a "denying" lifestyle will suffer very unpleasant consequences, losing rewards that could otherwise have been gained. The quality of his eternal life will be adversely affected.[10] A believer who has displayed a "confessing" lifestyle, however, will earn a commendation before the Father at the judgment seat of Christ, along with the rewards that will accompany it. He will have an "abundant" eternal life.

7

THE LEAST AND THE GREATEST

At the time of Christ, the Jews were hoping for the establishment of the Kingdom (foretold by the Old Testament prophets) under the personal reign of their Messiah. From Zacharias' statement at the time of Jesus' birth in Luke 1:71, to John the Baptist's proclamation in Matthew 3:2 (*"Repent, for the kingdom of heaven is at hand"*), to the disciples question in Acts 1:6 (*"Lord, will You at this time restore the kingdom to Israel?"*), this hope is expressed. Matthew's gospel, which was written primarily to the Jews, reveals further how this theocratic kingdom was legitimately offered by Jesus. Not only did He repeat the proclamation of John the Baptist, but went about the countryside preaching the "gospel of the kingdom."[1] (Matthew 4:23).

The Jews were not looking for a savior, but a ruling Messiah. After all, were they not God's chosen people? Did they not already understand the way of salvation? Did they not have the word of God in the law and the prophets? Wasn't a "devout Jew" justified before God?[2] The Jews expected, under this coming kingdom, that they would be more than citizens: they would rule alongside their Messiah. So absorbed with this idea were the disciples that they began to vie for positions of authority next to Jesus (Mark 10:35-45).

This, of course, led to their question: "Who then is the greatest in the kingdom of heaven?" (Matthew 18:1) In Jesus' answer that follows, it is important to remember that He is answering the disciples' question of ranking within His administration, and the character traits that are required for those who desire to serve under His rule. Jesus is not discussing justification or requirements for entry into eternal life.

Greatness and humility

> *Then Jesus called a little child to Him, set him in the midst of them, and said, "Assuredly, I say to you, unless you are converted and become as little children, you will by no means enter the kingdom of heaven. Therefore whoever humbles himself as this little child is the greatest in the kingdom of heaven." (Matthew 18:2-4)*

It is without question that the disciples were already believers at this point in the Gospel of Matthew, only days before Jesus' death. Jesus has just inferred that the disciples are "sons of the kingdom" in Matthew 17:24-27. When He uses the term "kingdom," Jesus is not referring to a place (like heaven), but His personal administration. In effect, He is saying, "If you want to serve under Me, you will need to change your prideful attitude and become humble, just like the little child here in My presence . . . for such are those who will assume the highest positions in My kingdom." "Entering into the kingdom" was

The Least And The Greatest

certainly understood by the disciples as "entering into their Messiah's administration."[3] The immediate context deals with the qualification (or lack of the same) to rule with Christ, as do other passages in the gospel accounts where Jesus refers to "greatness."

Two things should be noticed about the context of Matthew 18:2-4:

1. The disciples' question follows the unusual account of Jesus paying the temple tax for Himself and Peter:

   *When they had come to Capernaum, those who received the temple tax came to Peter and said, "Does your Teacher not pay the temple tax?" He said, "Yes." And when he had come into the house, Jesus anticipated him, saying, "What do you think, Simon? From whom do the kings of the earth take customs or taxes, from their sons or from strangers?" Peter said to Him, "From strangers." Jesus said to him, "Then the sons are free. Nevertheless, lest we offend [**skandalizō**] them, go to the sea, cast in a hook, and take the fish that comes up first. And when you have opened its mouth, you will find a piece of money; take that and give it to them for Me and you." (Matt. 17:24-27)*

   The Greek verb **skandalizō** means "to offend" or "cause to become offended," and *it is observed that every use of this verb in the gospels refers to offense taken with regard to the person or words of Jesus Christ.* The reason Jesus did not want to offend those who collected the temple tax was that many of the Jewish leaders were still open to His message and person.[4] The object lesson for Peter was this: <u>Though he had rights as a "son of the king," he was to humbly lay them aside5 to avoid being a stumbling block (an offense) to those who would believe in Jesus.</u>[6] It happens all too frequently that unbelievers reject the message of salvation because of offensive conduct by Christians! Such conduct is perhaps the greatest barrier to the growth of the kingdom of God[7] ... and could disqualify those who wish to rule with the Messiah.

2. The verses that immediately follow (Matthew 18:5-10) have a similar application: Those who want to rule with the Messiah must be careful not to cause new believers ("little ones" in 18:5-6) to become offended[8] (*skandalizō*) at the teachings or person of Jesus. This would cause "stumbling" and inhibit their maturity in the faith.

It is helpful here to elaborate on the uniqueness of the Greek verb *skandalizō*. The word does not mean "to sin" in the general sense of the word, but as mentioned above, points to a specific problem: *offense at the person or words of Jesus*. Paul says in Romans 14:13 that believers should not judge one another over disputed issues, being resolved not to cause a brother to fall (*skandalizō*); that is, to falter in the growth of their spiritual relationship with Christ. If one sees this from Jesus' standpoint, causing a brother to falter or stumble would be equivalent to causing His "bride" to be unfaithful, or to *take offense at her husband*. This would rightly invoke the disappointment of the groom. Paul felt this same frustration in 2 Corinthians 11:29: "*Who is weak, and I am not weak? Who is made to stumble, and I do not burn [with indignation]?*" This is such a serious issue that Jesus says it would be better for those who cause such stumbling to be drowned in the depths of the sea![9] It is a measure of our love for one another that we do not cause offense, for "*He who loves his brother abides in the light, and there is no cause for stumbling [skandalon] in him.*" (1 John 2:10)

If an unbeliever (Matthew 18:8-9) becomes offended (*skandalizō*)[10] at the words or person of Jesus, he might even refuse the offer of salvation! As believers, we should therefore make every effort to be as gracious as possible in presenting the salvation message, avoiding even the appearance of pride or a condescending attitude. As Jesus did in paying the temple tax, we are to avoid anything that might make the gospel offensive to unbelievers.

Greatness in the Sermon on the Mount

In Jesus' Sermon on the Mount, He describes the foundational moral dictates of His administration. In this case, the foundational principles do not reside in a constitution, but in the person of the Messiah, for He is the fulfillment of the law and the prophets. Chapters 5 through 7 of Matthew's gospel contain Jesus' standards of "kingdom righteousness," which are in stark contrast to those of the Jewish leadership (Matthew 5:20). His teachings are "lofty" and "demanding," yet this is exactly the plane of living to which He calls us.

> *"Do not think that I came to destroy the Law or the Prophets. I did not come to destroy but to fulfill. For assuredly, I say to you, till heaven and earth pass away, one jot or one tittle will by no means pass from the law till all is fulfilled. Whoever therefore breaks one of the least of these commandments, and teaches men so, shall be called <u>least</u> in the kingdom of heaven; but whoever does and teaches them, he shall be called <u>great</u> in the kingdom of heaven. For I say to you, that unless your righteousness exceeds the righteousness of the scribes and Pharisees, you will by no means enter the kingdom of heaven." (Matthew 5:17-20)*

In this passage from Matthew, Jesus is addressing Jews who are in a covenant relationship with God, and expect to enter the Messiah's kingdom. The term *"kingdom of heaven"* in this passage should not be equated with "eternal life in heaven", nor should "righteousness" be equated with 'imputed righteousness" (justification). Jesus is exhorting his listeners to have a *righteous lifestyle* that exceeds that of the scribes and Pharisees. The term "kingdom of heaven" would have been understood by the Jews in light of Daniel 2:44 as an *earthly kingdom set up by the God of heaven*. Jesus is setting the standard for those who desire to serve in His administration.

The Greek word for "breaks" in 5:19 is *lyō*, which means to annul, dismiss or subvert. The scribes and Pharisees placed their oral traditions and rituals above that of God's law. In this way they subverted its intent and diminished its force, and turned Judaism into an "offense." In Matthew chapters 6 and 7, Jesus exposes their subversion and hypocrisy in detail. Despite the exalted status which the scribes and Pharisees held among fellow Jews, Jesus says they will be the "least" in His administration, and perhaps not fit to rule whatsoever. Jesus would later say of them:

> *"But woe to you, scribes and Pharisees, hypocrites! For you shut up the kingdom of heaven against men; for you neither go in [yourselves], nor do you allow those who are entering to go in." (Matthew 23:13)*

> *"Woe to you, scribes and Pharisees, hypocrites! For you travel land and sea to win one proselyte, and when he is won, you make him twice as much a son of hell as yourselves." (Matthew 23:15)*

Greatness and a servant's heart

In Matthew 20:20-34[11], as with the prior passages, "greatness" is connected with ruling in the Messianic kingdom.

> *But Jesus called them to Himself and said, "You know that the rulers of the Gentiles lord it over them, and those who are great exercise authority over them. Yet it shall not be*

> *so among you; but whoever desires to become great among you, let him be your servant. And whoever desires to be first among you, let him be your slave – just as the Son of Man did not come to be served, but to serve, and to give His life a ransom for many." (Matthew 20:25-28)*

In contrast to Gentile rulers, with whom "greatness" is measured by the degree to which they exercise authority, those who assist Jesus in his administration will be considered "great" by the degree to which they serve others. They are to consider themselves as slaves (without rights), just as Christ gave up his "rights" to give His life a ransom for many. Paul elaborates beautifully on the character trait of selflessness in his letter to the church at Philippi:

> *Let nothing be done through selfish ambition or conceit, but in lowliness of mind let each esteem others better than himself. Let each of you look out not only for his own interests, but also for the interests of others. Let this mind be in you which was also in Christ Jesus, who, being in the form of God, did not consider it robbery to be equal with God, but made Himself of no reputation, taking the form of a bondservant, and coming in the likeness of men. And being found in appearance as a man, He humbled Himself and became obedient to the point of death, even the death of the cross. (Philippians 2:3-8)*

But not only do the Gentiles "lord it over" their subjects, so did the rulers of the Jews, who loved their titles and exalted positions. Jesus points out to his disciples in Matthew 23:11 that being a servant includes the willingness to be unrecognized and un-thanked by those who are being served.

In Luke 22:24-27 (parallel to Matthew 20:20-28), Jesus follows his teaching on greatness with a promise:

> "But you are those who have continued with Me in My trials. And I bestow upon you a kingdom, just as My Father bestowed one upon Me, that you may eat and drink at My table in My kingdom, and sit on thrones judging the twelve tribes of Israel." (Luke 22:28-30)

By "trials" Jesus means His testing. His disciples were being tested alongside their Master - and the test for "greatness" among them would not be passed until after His death. The reward promised for those who are found to be selfless is not only ruling with Christ, but fellowshipping with Him (eating at His table). It will be the sad consequence of leading selfish lives that many believers will forfeit such a great and wonderful privilege!

Following His exhortation on greatness in Matthew 20:20-28, Jesus leaves Jericho to encounter two blind men who loudly cry out "Have mercy on us, O Lord, Son of David!" (20:29-34). Here Jesus shows by example the very character trait He previously mentioned. In contrast to the multitude's desire to silence the blind men, Jesus has compassion on the blind men and restores their sight. To have a servant's heart, one must see others' needs as more important than his own, which requires a compassionate mindset. Compassion is often the "engine" that drives servanthood. Perhaps the primary reason many personal needs go unmet in churches today is a lack of compassion, coupled with a judgmental attitude. Both are seen in this brief encounter in Jesus' ministry.

Summary

The best employees of a company are those that are selfless, humble, and have compassion for their fellow workers. They will earn the company a good reputation. An owner would rank such employees as the greatest in his company and reward them accordingly. Conversely, those employees who are unprofitable, divisive, or tyrannical will reflect poorly on the company. They are apt to be demoted, moved to positions where they can do no further harm, or fired.

With government agencies, where the threat of being fired may be lessened, the temptation to be lazy, rude, or uncaring is increased. As many can testify, it is very frustrating to deal with public employees who act in these ways. This same temptation faces every Christian who believes in free grace and eternal security. Eternal security is not an excuse for offensive conduct that brings our employer (in this case, God) a bad reputation.

All of the Bible passages on "the least and the greatest" are connected to the Millennial government and ruling with Christ. While there is special application in Matthew's gospel for the Jews, there is also application for the Gentile believer, since the enduring saint is to co-rule with Christ (2 Timothy 2:12). "Greatness" in the coming kingdom will be measured by selflessness, humility, love for the brethren, and mercy with compassion. Believers exhibiting these character traits will fill the highest positions of authority in the kingdom.

8

ABIDING AND BURNING

At the moment a believer is adopted into the household of God, his eternal life begins. Thus, the *quality* of his eternal life is first experienced while he is yet in his sinful state. As our "Good Shepherd," Christ's desire is not only that we will enter into eternal life through Him, but that we will "go in and out and find pasture" (John 10:9). In the following verse, He restates this two-fold purpose: *"I have come that they may have life, and that they may have it more <u>abundantly</u>."* It is the *quality* of a believer's life that Satan wants to steal, kill and destroy. Christ could not have used stronger terms.

The abundant quality of eternal life *prior to one's death* is the subject of Jesus' exhortation on "abiding" and "burning" in John 15:1-11. Some unfortunately see this passage as a discourse on justification, and divide the subjects of the passage into two groups: the eternally condemned (cast from the vine and burned), and the eternally saved (those who abide in the vine). But such an explanation does not meet the test of good exegesis. There is a much better one, which has nothing to do with justification.

In John 15, Jesus eats His last meal with those He loves, and His words to his believing disciples (Judas having already left) convey a very personal message. His desire is that His disciples maintain <u>close fellowship</u> with Him, even after His death. To this end He calls them His friends, promises to send them the Holy Spirit and gives them His peace. One thing remains to ensure their survival and their ability to bear fruit in the world that hates them: <u>the disciples must abide in Him</u>. It is in the context of Jesus' desire that his disciples have an effective, fruitful walk that John 15:1-11 must be understood.

The terms "abiding" and "burning" describe opposites in believers: those who are in *intimate fellowship* with their Savior, and those who *resist* the call to be transformed into His likeness and purpose. It cannot be more strongly emphasized that unbelievers are not in view.[1] The principles set forth by Jesus in this passage are evident in God's relationship with Israel (past and present), as well as the Church He would establish. They are a repeated theme in both the gospels and epistles.

The significance of the true vine

> *"I am the true vine, and My Father is the vinedresser. Every branch in Me that does not bear fruit He takes away; and every branch that bears fruit He prunes, that it may bear more fruit. You are already clean because of the word which I have spoken to you. Abide in Me, and I in you. As the branch cannot bear fruit of itself, unless it abides in the vine, neither can you, unless you abide in Me." (John 15:1-4)*

Jesus says in John 15:1 that He is the <u>true</u>[2] <u>vine</u>[3]. To understand this Jewish metaphor, we must go back to the Old Testament. Israel was to be God's "pleasant vine". In planting the "vine" in the Promised Land, we learn from Isaiah 5:1-7 that God 1) prepared and maintained the ground, 2) built a tower in its midst, 3) made a winepress, 4) put a hedge around it, 5) built a wall around it, 6) pruned and tended it, and 7) caused it to be rained upon. These represents aspects of the privileges God granted to Israel in accordance with her exalted position and national calling. These privileges *were contingent upon Israel's obedience*. But in her idolatry and unfaithfulness, Israel brought forth "wild grapes." She did not remember her calling, she did not heed the warnings of the prophets, and she did not repent even as her divine protection was being removed! As a result, Israel lost her privileges, was uprooted by God and scattered among the nations of the world. Yet despite experiencing God's disfavor and being removed from the Promised Land, Israel *is still His treasured possession,*[4] though "buried"[5] and awaiting the appearance of her Messiah.

Being familiar with the law and prophets, the disciples surely saw in this discourse by Jesus the stark contrast between the "disobedient/false vine" (Israel) of Isaiah 5 and the Messiah they had followed for several years. Jesus was the "true vine" in the sense that He had been faithful and obedient to the Father's will (abiding in the Father) where the children of Israel had not. In being the true vine, Jesus was the fulfillment of the prophecy given in Isaiah 53:2, *"For He shall grow up before Him as a tender plant, and as a root out of dry ground."*[6] Further, the disciples would probably have understood this to mean that *only in Jesus* would the Jewish nation find fulfillment of her national destiny. Just as in the Abrahamic covenant, where the Jewish people were to be a blessing unto the Gentile world, Jesus (as the glory of the nation of Israel) was to be a "light unto the Gentiles" (Luke 2:32). "Abiding in the vine," then, is necessary to fulfilling a calling and bearing fruit (or "good grapes" as in Isaiah 5:4).

It must be remembered that Israel's position was attained <u>by grace through faith</u>, but the condition of her fellowship with God (and the privileges/blessings attached thereto) was maintained by obedience. This example is also seen in the person of Abram. His righteous position was attained by grace through faith;[7] while his privileges/blessings were contingent upon his obedience to God's command to leave his country and his kindred, and to dwell in the land God would show him.[8]

The branches

In studying John 15:1-11, one is immediately struck by the way Jesus describes the branches: they are in Him. This fact alone excludes the notion that unbelievers are in view in this passage. It is almost as if Jesus anticipated future attempts by some to twist the meaning of His words. One thing is sure: He did not want his *disciples* to misunderstand.

But we need not depend on this short prepositional phrase alone to confirm that this brief discourse is not about "saved" and "lost" individuals. These words of Jesus are uttered in a private room to his disciples only. Everyone in the upper room is a believer, for Judas has been sent away (John 13:27-30). Lest there be any question as to the remaining eleven, Jesus has already told them they are saved (". . . *and you are* clean, *but not all of you*" - John 13:10). He reaffirms this in his prayer for them in 17:12 (*"Those whom You gave Me I have kept; and* none of them is lost *except the son of perdition . . ."*), indicating that not only were the eleven all believers, but that their eternal security was His responsibility. Thus, the topic at hand is *not* how his disciples can become saved. Neither is Jesus explaining in this passage how his disciples can avoid losing eternal life; an interpretation that would be both unscriptural and a contradiction in terms.[9]

That the branches are "in him" indicates that at the moment a person first places his faith in Jesus for eternal life, he is in full fellowship with Jesus, having access to all the spiritual blessings and privileges "in the heavenlies".[10] He has, after all, responded in faith to the first and most important call upon his life. But though a new believer may have access to these blessings and privileges, his fruit-bearing capacity will depend upon obedience in his walk.

Abiding in the vine and bearing fruit

By the time we reach chapter 15 in John's gospel, Jesus is preparing his disciples for his departure, knowing within hours they will be left alone facing a formidable foe in a world that hates them (15:18-19). To be able to be fruitful disciples, love one another, and withstand persecution during His absence, Jesus tells them it is essential to "abide in Him":

> *"Abide in Me, and I in you. As the branch cannot bear fruit of itself, unless it abides in the vine, neither can you, unless you abide in Me. "I am the vine, you are the branches. He who abides in Me, and I in him, bears much fruit; for without Me you can do nothing." (John 15:4-5)*

Four times in these two short verses, the disciples are exhorted to "abide in Jesus". The concept of "abiding" did not originate with the upper room discourse. It can be found throughout the Old Testament in God's relationship with Israel. The Old Testament equivalent to "abiding" is "holding fast" (Hebrew *dabak*), as is found in Deuteronomy 10:20, *"You shall fear the Lord your God; you shall serve Him, and to Him you shall* hold fast . . ." Much like a parent who tells his young child to "stay close to me" when walking through a crowded public square, God wanted Israel to stay close so that they would enjoy His protection and His blessings. Only in staying close could they "bear fruit;" and only by clinging to Him could they fulfill their national destiny.[11]

It should be pointed out that the reward for "holding fast" for Israelites was not eternal life, but a myriad of earthly, temporal blessings[12] such as long life, dwelling securely and prosperously in the Promised Land, victory over enemies, and divine protection. Holding fast to God was indicative of a healthy and vibrant relationship: one exhibiting faithful obedience, by which the Israelites' love for God was measured. As long as they obeyed His statutes, they enjoyed their relationship with Him. More importantly, they were useable by God for His purposes when they held fast to Him.

This principle is no different for the believer today. One of the aspects of "holding fast" is obedience . . . and obedience is an integral part of intimate fellowship with Jesus. Jesus said, *"He who has My commandments and keeps them, it is he who* <u>*loves*</u> *Me."*[13] The apostle John (the disciple whom Jesus loved) enlarges upon this:

> *He who says, "I know Him,"*[14] *and does not keep His commandments, is a liar, and the truth is not in him. But whoever keeps His word, truly the love of God is perfected in him. By this we know that we are in Him. He who says he* <u>*abides*</u> *in Him ought himself also to walk just as He walked.* (1 John 2:4-6)

Staying close to Jesus necessarily involves walking as He walked, and "growing up in all things into Him who is the head – Christ."[15] This includes maturing in faith, virtue, knowledge, self-control, perseverance, godliness, brotherly kindness and love,[16] all of which require some degree of dying to self;[17] without which the fruitfulness of a believer is hampered. It is not automatic that a believer will produce fruit simply because he is saved. This is clear not only from Jesus' use of the word "if" in John 15:6-7, but passages such as 2 Peter 1:8-10, 1 John 1:6 and 1 John 2:4.

Increasing the productivity of the branches

In 15:2, Jesus says that the Father (the Vinedresser) "prunes" (NKJV) every branch that is in Him, so that it may bear more fruit. The Greek word **kathairō**, however, is probably better translated "cleans," as in the cleaning from impurities or filthiness. This relates directly to the prior words of Jesus to His disciples in John 13:8, *"If I do not wash you, you have no part with Me,"* and in 13:9, *"He who is bathed needs only to wash his feet, but is completely clean . . ."* Here the emphasis is on daily confession for cleansing of unrighteousness, so that a believer's fellowship with Jesus (abiding in Him) is not impaired.

> *"If we say we have no sin, we deceive ourselves and the truth is not in us. If we confess our sins, He is faithful and just to forgive us our sins and to* <u>cleanse</u> *us from all unrighteousness." (1 John 1:8-9)*

While one's justification does not need maintenance, Jesus desires that we *maintain our fellowship* with Him on a daily basis. If sins are not regularly confessed, and one's course reset through the "washing of God's word" (John 15:3), hardening of heart and bitterness can result. This is pictured in married life, as well, where the enactment of the marriage ceremony does not, in itself, guarantee a joyful relationship. For a joyful marriage, daily "maintenance" is required.[18] In the metaphor Jesus uses in John 15, washing was needed to remove parasites and other destructive organisms from the vine. This involved regular inspection of leaves and branches, especially those parts not receiving light, where damage can occur unnoticed.

It should be noted that failure to bear fruit does not immediately result in judgment. In 15:2, Jesus says, *"Every branch in Me that does not bear fruit He takes away . . ."* (NKJV). The translation "takes away" (*airō*) in this verse is probably better translated "lifted up" (as in Luke 17:13, John 11:41 and Acts 4:24), and especially in the context of caring for a vineyard, where parts of the vines can sag onto the ground below. This indicates that the Father does everything possible to allow believers to become fruit bearing. He exposes them to the light of His word and the testimony of fellow believers.[19] Those who continue in darkness after being saved are "lifted up" into the light that they might yet abide in the vine and be productive.

Failing to abide in the vine and being cast out

Failure to abide and bear fruit in spite of the Father's efforts to transform a believer's life has serious consequences. Jesus warns:

> *"If anyone does not abide in Me, he is cast out as a branch and is withered; and they gather them and throw them into the fire, and they are burned."* (John 15:6)

1) <u>Being cast out.</u> The initial consequence of failing to abide in the vine is a loss of fellowship or closeness to the Lord. Lest there be any question about whether these are believers, Jesus says they are cast out *as branches*. Being cast from the vine, in this instance, is to be cast from a place of blessing and privilege *in this earthly life*.[20] Note again the privileges of being "in the vine" in John 15:1-11: answered prayer, the bearing of fruit, enjoyment of the relationship, and glorification of the Father. Thus, when a believer does *not* abide, his prayers are hindered,[21] he fails to bear fruit,[22] he loses joy,[23] and the Father is put to open shame instead of glorified.[24] None of these include the loss of eternal life. Eternal life is neither a blessing nor a privilege, contingent upon obedience. It is a *gift*.

A similar situation is observed in the life of David after he had his affair with Bathsheba. In Psalm 51, he pleads:

> *"Do not cast me away from Your presence, and do not take Your Holy Spirit from me. Restore to me the joy of Your*

salvation, and uphold me by Your generous Spirit." (Psalm 51:11-12)

It is clear that David was not at risk of losing his justification, nor was his prayer an attempt to regain it. His plea was entirely concerned with regaining the <u>joy</u> of being saved, of being in the presence of the Lord, and experiencing the blessings that follow. As for the nation of Israel, being "cast out" meant removal of her prominence among nations and loss of her divine protection.

But there is more to being removed from the vine than mere separation. These fruitless branches are <u>cast out</u>. This is a deliberate action taken for the benefit of the fruit-bearing branches; for the presence of a fruitless branch will eventually impair the productivity of those that remain in the vine. Thus, the blessings and privileges that would have been available to those that are cast out are now given to those that abide. This has an eschatological parallel seen in several of Jesus' parables.[25] Furthermore, not only do fruitless branches take up valuable space in the vine, they work *against* the purposes of the Vinedresser, whose goal is to have the most fruitful vineyard possible.[26] The apostle Paul, in referring to worldly believers, said, *"For many walk, of whom I have told you often, and now tell you even weeping, that they are the* <u>enemies of the cross of</u> <u>Christ</u>*: whose end is destruction, whose god is their belly, and whose glory is in their shame—who set their mind on earthly things."*[27] Satan surely knows that if a new believer can be "neutralized," not only would his fruit-bearing capability be eliminated, he can become a tool to bring disgrace the gospel and hinder the fruit-bearing of faithful believers! It is no wonder that such branches are cast out.

2) <u>Withering.</u> The second consequence of failing to abide is seen in the withering of the branch. This is a natural consequence of being separated from (not abiding in) the source of life. Psalm 1 infers that if a believer's life is not "planted" by the source of

living water (Jesus), his "leaf will wither" and not be fruitful. The same Hebrew word (here translated "fade") is found in Isaiah 64:6-7:

> *"But we are all like and unclean thing, and our righteousnesses are like filthy rags; we all* <u>fade</u> *as a leaf, and our iniquities, like the wind, have taken us away. And there is no one who calls on Your name, who stirs himself up to take hold of You; for You have hidden Your face from us, and have* <u>consumed</u> *us because of our iniquities."*

Among the seeds that are sown in Matthew 13:5-6 is the one that springs up in shallow soil. It represents a shallowness of commitment and love for Christ. Such a disciple will "wither" or stumble when faced with hard times or persecution . . . the consequence of failing to abide.

3) <u>Being gathered and burned.</u> The "burning" in John 15 is a judgment on the willful disobedience of a believer. It is the destruction "by fire" of the unfruitful, unrepentant parts of a believer's life. In fact, it does not appear that the purpose of the "burning" is to bring about repentance,[28] even though repentance could occur. Nor does it appear that this "burning" is a purifying fire, in which the "dross" of a believer's life is removed in this life. *Rather, the fact that a withered branch is burned indicates the utter worthlessness of an unfruitful life to God, and the worthlessness of all works done in the flesh.* This worthlessness is depicted in Matthew 5:13, when a believer loses his "saltiness" and is good for nothing except to be trampled underfoot by men . . . and in Luke 3:9, where *". . . every tree that does not bear good fruit is cut down and thrown into the fire."*

It must be emphasized that this "burning" is not the destruction (or eternal condemnation) of the individual believer, but of the aspects of his life that are worthless to the plan and purpose of God. Of this, the person of Lot in the Old Testament serves as a type. He "moved his tent toward

Sodom,"[29] indicating his love for the world. In the end we see that, though Lot was a believer, his family was threatened by the godless men with which Lot kept company, and all to which he had dedicated his life "went up in smoke".

This "burning" indicates not only destruction that can be experienced during a believer's earthly life (the trampling of one's fruitless life by the world), but loss at the judgment seat of Christ. Here every believer will give an account of his actions from the time at which he became saved (and betrothed) to the time he dies or is caught up in the rapture. All unrighteous works with which believers have "clothed" themselves will be consumed by fire. This will leave some standing shamefully naked before their Groom.[30]

Before Jesus begins His rule during the Millennium, He will also burn up all things that are worthless or unrighteous *on the earth*. Those who become believers during the Tribulation will enter the Millennium as servants of Christ, but their lives will not have been examined with the raptured Church at the judgment seat of Christ. Thus, their worthless works (along with all unbelievers who survive the Tribulation) will be destroyed when Christ begins His reign. Note the warning given in Matthew 13:41-42, related to the end of this age:

> "The Son of Man will send out His angels, and they will gather out of His kingdom <u>all things that offend</u>, and those who practice lawlessness, and will cast them into the furnace of fire. There will be wailing and gnashing of teeth."

The "weeping and gnashing of teeth" mentioned above probably applies to the believers who survived the Tribulation, who only now realize the extent of their loss in not receiving the gospel message by faith earlier.[31] The word "offend" (***skandalon***) in these verses is typically connected to the person or teachings of Jesus wherever it is found in the New Testament, as in 1 John 2:9-10:

> He who says he is in the light, and hates his brother, is in darkness until now. He who loves his brother abides in the light, and there is no cause for stumbling [**skandalon**] in him.

That which is cast into the fiery furnace along with those who "practice lawlessness" (unbelievers) at the beginning of the Millennium are those things that "cause offense" to the person or teachings of Jesus.

Summary

In summary, John 15:1-11 is not a passage on justification, but fellowship with Christ in this life. Jesus calls all believers to abide in Him, in all that He has taught, modeled, promised, and provided. *Only by abiding in Him will a life be made fruitful, abundant and joyful.* Some believers, however, will fail to abide after having been saved. This is directly related to a willful rejection of the upward call of God in Christ Jesus; the chief manifestation of which is the inability to produce fruit.[32] Such fruitless lives fall under the temporal wrath of God. Being cast out, they wither like branches removed from their source of life. Failing to endure persecution and being choked by the cares of this world, their lives ultimately become worthless to the plan and purpose of God. In this condition some believers will appear at the judgment seat of Christ in a shameful state: *saved*, but only as through fire.

> "And now, little children, abide in Him, that when He appears, we may have confidence and not be ashamed before Him at His coming." (1 John 2:28)

> "Therefore, since we are receiving a kingdom which cannot be shaken, let us have grace, by which we may serve God acceptably with reverence and godly fear. For our God is a consuming fire." (Hebrews 12:28-29)[33]

As sad as this will be for many, the sadder truth is that such a shameful appearance before our Groom will have negative consequences related to opportunities, responsibilities and intimacy of fellowship in the coming age.

With the persecution of believers increasing worldwide in the last decade, the need to abide in Jesus is greater than ever. But with increasing persecution comes even greater opportunities to bear fruit, and to experience the joy of Christ (John 15:11) in full measure. Would that every believer know this truth, and seek the abundant life Jesus promises!

EPILOGUE

When I was first introduced to the Biblical passages on rewards and the judgment seat of Christ, and read of Paul "running to win the prize", I couldn't help seeing the picture of the proverbial carrot in front of the donkey, put there as an enticement to get him to move. Is that what God is doing for the believer? Do we really need rewards to encourage us to forge ahead in our Christian walk? And I remember thinking, *"Isn't it self-serving to pursue awards in eternal life?"* Furthermore, if seeking rewards is a selfish pursuit, how can it be that one of the character traits on which rewards are to be distributed is *selflessness*? Yet, it is indisputable that Jesus has put the "carrot" before each believer.

In time, it occurred to me that the "carrot" was not to be understood in worldly terms. It was not mundane, as rewards in this life typically are. The "carrot" Jesus puts before every believer is actually *Himself*. It is a deeper, closer, more fulfilling and enjoyable relationship with Him in eternity. Every reward, whether crown, position of authority, new name, dazzling robe, or other privilege, is representative of this deeper relationship. They are all *from* Him and *of* Him. Simply put, every reward is *more of Jesus* and *more of life* in eternity. This fuller relationship, this richer quality of eternal life, is available to all who are in Christ . . . and it is His desire that we enter into it.

But though the goal is simple to describe, the pursuit is not. We are called to set sail out into the open ocean, into uncharted waters where there are storms to be weathered, enemies to be defeated and other perils to be faced that are too numerous to mention. Some believers start out well, but allured by the siren song of the world, stray off course and shipwreck their faith. Other believers never even leave port. At a great cost they have been entrusted with a sea worthy and fully-equipped vessel. They are blessed with an ebb tide and favorable wind, yet they settle for the comforts of shore life. It is difficult to imagine the greatness of their loss!

It is by faith that we set out on this journey. Often the actual destination (as it was for Abraham) is unclear. It is not a journey for the faint of heart, but for the faithful of heart. It is by faith that we learn to navigate and keep our ship on course; that we achieve victory in battle; that we reach our destination; and above all, that we experience the joy of getting to know the Owner and Master of the ship, *who happens to reside onboard.*

As Paul says in Romans 11:22, our God is "good and severe". *Both* goodness and severity are to be experienced in the life of a believer. To assign God's severity only to non-believers is to fail to see much of His plan and purpose for life; and to fail to be shaped by the hand of the Potter. It often takes the entire journey of one's life to realize that these two facets are inextricably linked: one cannot be understood apart from the other. This link is so profound, that Paul would exclaim just a few verses later,

> *Oh the depth of the riches both of the wisdom and knowledge of God! How unsearchable are His judgments and His ways past finding out!*

"For who has known the mind of the Lord?
Or who has become His counselor?"
"Or who has first given to Him
And it shall be repaid to Him?"
For of Him and through Him and to Him are all things, to whom be glory forever. Amen. (Romans 11:33-36)

END NOTES

Preface

1. The words "outer darkness" (NKJV) appear only in Matthew's gospel. See Matthew 8:12, 22:13 and 25:30.

2. It is probable that the expression "birds of the air" in this parable has the same meaning as in the parable of the sower and the seed (Matthew 13:3-9).

3. A mustard plant was usually found in a garden (not in a field), and would have been pruned so that it did not grow to the size of a tree. That this particular mustard plant has grown so large that birds come and nest in its branches indicates the unrestrained growth of "visible Christendom" in this current age. Several of the epistles bear witness to the intrusion of false doctrine and hypocrisy into the Church from the very beginning. It has also been evident that over the past 2,000 years, many have made the Church their home for reasons other than spiritual rebirth.

4. "Leaven", when used metaphorically in Scripture, typically denotes hypocrisy. See Matthew 16:6-12, Mark 8:15, Luke 12:1, 1 Corinthians 5:6-9 and Galatians 5:9.

5. Entire chapters in the gospels are devoted to discipleship. See Matthew chapters 10, 18 & 25, for example, along with significant portions of other chapters in this gospel alone.

6. "Free gift" (free grace) is a term introduced by Paul in Romans 5:15, 16 and 17 (NKJV). It is redundant in that a "gift" is, by definition, already free. In being redundant, Paul is stressing the fact that justification (imputed righteousness) is *absolutely free*: it costs the believer nothing. Perhaps Paul anticipated the effort to undermine this fundamental truth using "perseverance justification".

7. Ananias and Sapphira in Acts 5:1-11, and the believer in 1 Corinthians 5:1-5 are familiar examples.

8. See Romans 6. Paul argues in 6:13 that it is possible for a believer to let sin master him after being justified ("Therefore do not let sin reign in your mortal body so that you obey its evil desires"). The consequences of a believer allowing sin to reign in his life is stated in 6:23 as a "daily ration of death". Note that the Greek word for "wages", ***opsōnion***, refers to a daily allowance of food given to a Roman soldier in lieu of money. In Romans 6:23 Paul is not referring to eternal damnation.

Chapter 1

1. This is also known as the Bema Seat judgment, as Paul uses the Greek word ***bēma*** in 2 Corinthians 5:10. Paul is referring to the official seat used by those who judged athletic events in his day, where rewards were given to those who competed well.

2. According to John 5:24, a person is given eternal life (is justified) at the moment of belief; not at some later date. The judgment seat of Christ represents the personal inspection of His "bride" for deeds done during her time of betrothal; and takes place at least 1,000 years prior to the great white throne judgment.

3. Since previous resurrections of the righteous (Old Testament and New Testament saints) have already taken place prior to, or at the beginning of, the Millennium, it is likely that only the unrighteous dead remain for this judgment. See the prophetic time line at the end of this chapter.

4. If believers and unbelievers are grouped together at the Great White Throne Judgment (Rev. 20:11-15), the only apparent thing distinguishing the two groups from one another is the quality of their works. Thus, being found in the Book of Life would erroneously be connected to works, not belief.
5. Most all of the warnings contained in the epistles are directed at believers. If one assumes these warnings apply to unbelievers as well as believers, then loss of rewards at the judgment seat of Christ will be misconstrued to mean loss of eternal life.
6. Some who have written commentaries on 1 Corinthians 9:27 forget that judging a race is more than merely handing out ribbons or trophies to winners. It is a race official's responsibility to see that the events are run fairly, without partiality to any competitor. If a runner is judged to have impeded or hindered the progress of a fellow competitor, for example, he may be disqualified by the race official, resulting in a loss of potential recognition and honor. Christ is the "race official" in a believer's life.
7. "Adversaries" or "enemies" in Hebrews 10:27 is the Greek word **hupenantios**, meaning "contrary" or "against," as in Colossians 2:14, the only other time it appears in the New Testament. If a believer's life is lived contrary to the will of God, he will be treated accordingly at the judgment seat of Christ. Disobedient believers are not "enemies" in the sense of Matthew 5:44 ("Love your enemies . . .") and Luke 20:43 (". . . til I make Your enemies Your footstool"), where the Greek word is **ekthros**.
8. See Ephesians 4:30 and 1 Thessalonians 5:19.
9. See Numbers 15:30-31.
10. See Galatians 3:10-13.
11. It can be argued that the "wrath" of God, when expressed in its active form in the New Testament, is always temporal, and experienced in an earthly, not eternal, setting. When directed at believers, God's wrath is typically intended to bring about

repentance. (See Ephesians 5:6, Colossians 3:6, 1 Thessalonians 5:9, Hebrews 3:11 and 4:3) The purpose of turning over the sexually-immoral believer in 1 Corinthians 5:5 to Satan for the "destruction of the flesh" was to cause repentance so that something of his earthly life would be preserved at the judgment seat of Christ.

12. The warning of Jesus in Matthew 5:13 about saltiness and the exhortation to "let your light shine before men" relate to the circumstance of persecution in 5:11-12. Failure to "shine before men" in the midst of persecution results in a lost opportunity to bear fruit. See Matthew 13:5-6. All believers are "salt", but not all are "salty".

13. See John 8:11.

Chapter 2

1. The Millennial Kingdom (see Revelation 20:4) is often ignored because it has not been understood by a number of mainline Christian denominations as a literal 1,000-year period of time where Jesus actually reigns on the earth. Yet this exact time period is mentioned six times in Revelation 20! Since this kingdom has been so often "spiritualized", the Bible passages relating to it (in both the OT and NT) tend either to be minimized or misapplied.

2. See Ezekiel 36:33-38.

3. See Luke 19:15-19, Revelation 20:4.

4. Not only will much of the earth's population will perish during the Tribulation (Revelation 6:7-8 and 9:18), but all unrighteous persons remaining at the time of Jesus' return to reign (Matthew 25:31-46).

5. See Psalm 2:7-9, Revelation 2:27, 12:5, 19:15, 20:4.

6. See Matthew 25:21.

7. See Matthew 20:16 and 22:14.

8. It is probable that not all Christians are "**called** to the wedding supper of the Lamb" (Revelation 19:9). It is a reward for faithfulness to be invited, and happy (blessed) are those who are called. But some will weep at being denied the privilege. (See Matthew 22:11-14.)

9. See Chapter 6 – "Confessing and Denying" for a full explanation of 2 Timothy 2:11-13.

10. See chapter on "The First and the Last" for a full explanation of Matthew 20:1-16.

11. See chapter on "Robes and Wedding Garments" for a full explanation of Matthew 22:1-14.

Chapter 3

1. God surely does wipe away all tears (Revelation 21:4), but not until the eternal age. In the Millennium preceding the eternal age, Christ will rule over the sinful nature of men with an "iron scepter" (Psalms 2:9, Revelation 2:27), and must deal with one final rejection of His sovereignty (Revelation 20:7-9).

2. The term "eternal life" can sometimes mean "a life of eternal value," where the emphasis is not on the timeless aspect, but on the quality aspect of eternal life. Romans 6:23 is a good example of a verse where the true meaning of the term "eternal life" is often overlooked. When Paul says, "the wages of sin is death," he is not referring to hell, but to the destructive, fruitless, ineffective quality of a carnal lifestyle. The entirety of chapter 6 concerns deliverance from the power of sin in one's walk with Christ. ("Therefore do not let sin reign in your mortal body, that you should obey its lusts." – 6:12) Thus, when Paul writes, "the gift of God is eternal life," he is not referring to heaven, but to the eternal value or quality of a life lived in Jesus Christ.

3. See chapter on "The Gift and the Inheritance".

4. The context in Matthew 19:16 – 20:28 is entirely about discipleship. It has been claimed by some that the "denarius" represents justification (or eternal life), but such cannot be the case since it was paid as a wage.

5. The text reads that the owner agreed with the laborers, indicating the proposal originated with them. Moreover, the parable fails to make a relevant point in addressing Peter's question if the owner initiated the idea of a contract for a fixed wage.

6. Some would argue that all laborers were paid the same; but there can be no question that the workers hired at the eleventh hour were paid twelve times the hourly wage of those hired at daybreak. It is telling that the "contract laborers" felt they had been paid less, for such was the reason for their envy and accusation against the master of the vineyard.

7. The Pharisee in this story may well have already been justified. Regular confession of specific sins, while necessary for cleansing and fellowship, is not required for positional righteousness. This is the message of John 13:10, where the disciples (except Judas Iscariot) were said only to need their feet washed, being that they had already taken a bath (had already been declared righteous).

8. In the prior chapter, Jesus says of those who come to sit down to eat **in the kingdom of God**, ". . . there are last who will be first, and there are first who will be last." (Luke 13:29-30)

9. The Greek word translated "rubbish" in Philippians 3:8 actually means "dung." Thus, Paul meant that his pedigree was not only worthless in contributing to his life of righteousness, it was **offensive** to God!

10. Note the connection with Luke 14:12-14 in this regard. A person might not accept an invitation to a dinner if he felt that he might be obliged in return. It is possible that those refusing the invitation were self-righteousness, and felt little sense of "indebtedness" to Jesus, who not only gave his life to save them, but lives to intercede for them. As a result, they felt little compulsion to live a selfless

life. It is in this way that they refused the invitation (calling) of God. Their excuses are not only lame; they are that which testify to their backward priorities in living the Christian life.

11. See also Matthew 22:11-14, where the guest without a wedding garment (righteous works) is denied the privilege of eating at the same event.

Chapter 4

1. See Ephesians 1:14 and Colossians 1:12.
2. Jacob blesses Joseph by giving Ephraim and Manasseh full status as sons. Thus, what would have been the "tribe of Joseph" now becomes the "tribe of Ephraim" and the "tribe of Manasseh". Thirteen tribes entered the Promised Land. All had a land inheritance except the tribe of Levi, whose inheritance was the Lord Himself.
3. Paul also uses **epilambanomai** in 1 Timothy 6:18-19, where it is connected to storing up a good foundation for eternal life by doing good works in this life.
4. That Jesus tells the parable of the good Samaritan to answer the lawyer's question is further evidence that the issue under discussion in 10:23 is not "how to gain eternal life". It is apparent that the lawyer, by seeking to "justify himself" (be assured that his current obedience to the Mosaic law was sufficient), had a poor understanding of what it meant to love his neighbor as himself. The priest and the Levite surely had what they thought were "justifiable" reasons to avoid the man left for dead by the robbers; but their actions were indicative of a lack of love for others . . . and correspondingly, a lack of love for God. (See 1 John 4:20-21.)
5. The man in the Mark passage is identified as a rich young ruler in the parallel account found in Matthew 19:16. It is entirely possible, due to the man's youth, that his wealth was inherited.

6. See Romans 3:20.
7. See the parallel passage in Mark 10:17-22.
8. Had the issue been justification, it would seemingly be cruel of Jesus to send away the young man with no answer; or even worse, with the idea that justification must be earned. The man went away sad because of the high cost of committed discipleship, not the cost of justification, which is a free gift.
9. See Luke 9:57-62, Matthew 13:7, 22, Philippians 3:18-19, and 1 Timothy 6:9, 17.
10. The camel was the largest of animals designated "unclean" to the Israelites (see Leviticus 11:4). "Uncleanness," furthermore, pictures the status of an Israelite's walk and his fellowship with God, not the status of his justification.
11. The word "salvation" (*sōtēria*) used in Hebrews 1:14 is repeated in 2:3, 2:10, 6:9 and 9:28. In all cases it refers to the perfecting of believers' lives with a view of their inheritance in mind; a concept first introduced in 1:4, regarding the excellent name inherited by Jesus. The major warnings in the epistle are similarly related to this topic, as evidenced by 6:12 and the example of Esau given in 12:16-17.
12. Inheriting the kingdom of God should not be confused with becoming justified. Clearly Paul is warning Christians, not unbelievers, in Galatians 5. See also 1 Corinthians 6:9-10, where Paul warns that the "unrighteous" (**adikos**) shall not inherit the kingdom of God. While **adikos** can sometimes refer to the unsaved, in this passage it likely describes those brethren who are acting in an unjust, sinful, or deceitful manner.
13. Also see Matthew 5:10, *"Blessed are those who are persecuted for righteousness' sake, for theirs is the kingdom of heaven."* The term "kingdom of heaven" would most likely have been understood by Jews as the literal Messianic Kingdom on earth, due to the prophetic dream given to Nebuchadnezzar in Daniel

2. In particular, see Daniel 2:34-35, and 2:44, where the "God of heaven" sets up a kingdom that shall stand forever.

14. Also see Matthew 13:5-6, 20-21. These seeds that landed on rocky ground represent believers, for they sprung to life (germinated). However, they failed to produce fruit, being unable to endure persecution and trials. (Unbelievers cannot produce fruit for the kingdom of God, nor are they exhorted to endure persecution for Christ.)

15. In the Old Testament Hosea is commanded by God to take a harlot for a wife; symbolic of Israel who "playing the harlot" (Hosea 1:2) by worshipping idols. Israel's continued rebellion and lack of repentance led to God's judgment of Israel by the nations of Assyria and Babylon. The tribes of Dan and Ephraim seem to have fallen so far into idolatry that their names are missing from the list of faithful tribes in Revelation 7:4-8. Could it be that these two tribes lost their Millennial inheritance due to idol worship? God says of Ephraim, *"Woe to them, for they have fled from Me! Destruction to them, because they have transgressed against Me! Though I redeemed them, yet they have spoken lies against Me. Though I disciplined and strengthened their arms, yet they devise evil against Me; they return, but not to the Most High . . ."* (Hosea 7:13, 15-16a). See also Ezekiel 16:15ff.

16. Compare to Matthew 22:13. See Chapter 5 for a fuller explanation of "outer darkness".

17. Corruption (***phthora***) conveys the idea of decay and corrosion, not eternal damnation.

18. Neither the context nor the wording of the parable indicates that the rich man was condemned to hell for his love of wealth. The message of the parable is directed to believers as a warning against being obsessed with earthly possessions. It is not directed at the unbelieving rich, for their lives cannot be justified by selling what they have to give alms (Luke 12:33). Justification cannot be purchased; it is appropriated as a free gift.

19. See Genesis 15:1, Matthew 5:5, Hebrews 6:12, 1Peter 3:8-9, Revelation 21:7. In Genesis 15:1, Abraham is rewarded by God for his faithfulness. In the Hebrew language, the word of the Lord in 15:1 literally reads, *"Do not be afraid, Abram. I am your shield. Your reward is exceedingly great."*

Chapter 5

1. The first mention of Christ in this regard is found in Genesis 3:20, when Adam (by faith) named his wife the "mother of life." The name "Eve" sprung directly from 3:15, where her "seed" was to be the Life and Light of men (John 1:4). In response to Adam's faith, God provides them with "robes of righteousness."
2. Jesus uses the metaphor of a Jewish wedding in John 14:2-3 and Luke 12:35-40.
3. The parable is set up by Jesus' declaration in Matthew 21:31, "Assuredly, I say to you that tax collectors and harlots enter the kingdom of God before you."
4. Similarly, in Psalm 51:11 David seeks not to be cast away from God's presence. His fear is not loss of justification, but loss of fellowship.
5. The term "outer darkness" is more properly translated, "the darkness outside." The emphasis here is not so much on a particular place the man is cast, but on the loss of the privilege of dining with the other guests, who are all properly attired. Jewish wedding banquets traditionally took place at night, thus denial of entry would leave a person in the "darkness outside."
6. "Weeping and gnashing of teeth" signifies great remorse, but does not in itself imply a condition of hell. Esau similarly wept at his lost blessing (Hebrews 12:17), a result of treating it as a common thing (Hebrews 10:29) during his life. In Matthew 24:51, the unfaithful servant is "cut to pieces," and placed with the hypocrites, where there is "weeping and gnashing of teeth." This figurative language illustrates both remorse and anguish.

7. ***Dikaioma*** is found but ten times in the N.T. In Romans 5:18 the word is used to mean the "righteous act" of Christ (his obedient death on the cross), by which the free gift of justification came to all who believe.
8. The man is called "friend" by his king; he is cast from a wedding banquet, not from the kingdom; he is one of the "called" of Jesus Christ (see Romans 1:6), but not one of the chosen.
9. Here the term "naked" (***gymnos***) likely means "ill clad" or "without an outer garment," as in John 21:7.
10. The Greek word ***skybalon*** ("dung") is often incorrectly translated "rubbish" or "trash;" perhaps an effort by translators to use a more polite English word. But such a translation misses the repugnance and offensiveness to God that Paul intended to convey with regard to living his life while placing confidence in the flesh. Paul's theme in Philippians is not justification, but living selflessly.
11. Bartimaeus had placed his faith in Jesus, and was justified, well before he received his sight.
12. The most valuable pearls are those initiated without any human intervention whatsoever (as opposed to cultured pearls). Significant and beautiful ones are rare indeed, and involve many thin layers of deposited calcium carbonate. The more layers of covering, the greater the depth of the pearl's beauty and radiance becomes.
13. The emphasis in Matthew 6:19-34 is on righteous living, not believing unto justification. How we serve God in this age affects our "clothing" in the next.
14. See James 1:27.
15. Matthew 5:16.
16. See Acts 22:23-26. A Roman citizen could not be beaten prior to his trial (if arrested), nor could he be tortured. If found guilty of a crime deserving death; he could not be crucified. Thus Paul,

being a Roman citizen, was beheaded, while Peter (who was not a Roman citizen) was crucified.

17. David R. Anderson, *We Believe in Eternal Security,* (unpublished pamphlet, c. 1991), p. 22-23.

18. Is it possible that the "Book of Life" contains more than simply a list of names of those who have eternal life? Might it include eternal rewards that are assigned on an individual basis: eternal positions of authority, roles, privileges, and other aspects of the quality of eternal life that have been laid up for believers? To have a person's name "stricken from the Book of Life" would then indicate that certain individuals (those who do not overcome, for example) lose rewards that would otherwise have been granted.

19. See Chapter 6 - "Confessing and Denying." In Matthew 10, Jesus elaborates on the cost of discipleship. He will someday commend to the Father those who were willing to pay the cost, whose lifestyles openly displayed the grace they have received and unashamedly confessed Christ as Lord. However, Jesus will not commend to the Father those believers who have shrunk back due to persecution, ridicule and trials, and whose lifestyles have been compromised by worldliness. See also the parable of the sower in Matthew 13:3-9.

20. Though the Church is collectively the "bride of Christ" (2 Cor. 11:2, Eph. 5:25-27, Rev. 19:7, 21:9), an individual application of the typology set forth in a Jewish marriage is suggested in a number of Jesus' parables.

Chapter 6

1. "In the ancient world there was no banking system as we know it today, and no paper money. All money was made from metal, heated until liquid, poured into moulds and allowed to cool. When the coins were cooled, it was necessary to smooth off the uneven edges. The coins were comparatively soft, and of course

many people shaved them closely. In one century, more than eighty laws were passed in Athens to stop the practice of whittling down the coins then in circulation. But some money-changers were men of integrity, who would accept no counterfeit money; they were men of honor who put only genuine, full-weight money into circulation. Such men were called **dokimos**, and this word is used here for the Christian as he is to be seen by the world." (Donald Grey Barnhouse, *Romans: God's Glory*, p. 18.)

2. In 2 Timothy 2:13, the literal reading of the Greek is, *"If we <u>do not believe</u>..."* Some translations improperly insert here the adjective *faithless*, which diminishes the full force of this verse. The Greek verb **apisteō** clearly denotes an effort on the part of the individual to reject his faith, or to stop believing, after having been saved.

3. See Chapter 1 – The Lamb and the Judge.

4. See Matthew 7:24.

5. If there could be said to be an example of a believer forsaking his faith in Christ, this would be it. If Peter did not lose eternal life at this point, having <u>utterly</u> denied (**aparneomai**) Jesus, then how could those who deny (**arneomai**) Jesus to a lesser extent in Matthew 10:33 become lost?

6. In John 10:28-30, Jesus says, *"And I give them [His sheep] eternal life, and they shall never perish; neither shall anyone snatch them out of My hand. My Father, who has given them to Me, is greater than all; and no one is able to snatch them out of My Father's hand. I and My Father are one."* Should a believer be capable of losing his salvation (eternal life), it could not be said that God is omnipotent.

7. See Romans 8:34 and Hebrews 7:25.

8. See Matthew 26:75 and John 21:15-19.

9. Under the Mosaic Law, there was an offering proscribed for unintentional sin, but not for presumptuous sin (see Numbers 15:30). Presumptuous sin is sin committed with the attitude

that God will forgive it anyway. This is exactly the attitude that Paul decries in Romans 6:1 . . ."*Shall we continue in sin that grace may abound?*" There was no sacrifice under the Mosaic Law that would restore fellowship with God in such a case. In other words, if one lives a life of intentional sin thinking that God will look the other way, he is mistaken. The works done in such a life are subject to physical destruction; but the believer's justification is always secure.

10. See Chapter 4 – "The Gift and the Inheritance."

Chapter 7

1. The "gospel of the kingdom" should not be equated with the "gospel of salvation" in Romans 1:16. The good news (gospel) that Jesus preached in Matthew 4 was that the kingdom of God was at hand. (See Matthew 12:28, Luke 10:9, 11) It had nothing to do with salvation through His death and resurrection.

2. In all dispensations of history, man has been saved by faith. However, the object of faith was not Jesus Christ until His first coming. Such "devout Jews" as Simeon (Luke 2:25) and those in Acts 2:5 surely would have stood justified before God has they died prior to knowing of Jesus' sacrifice for their sins. Of course, not all Jews were saved in Jesus' day, since their faith was not in God, but in themselves. Jesus became the true test of where a Jew had placed his faith. (See John 8:42.)

3. Conversely, the disciples would have understood failure to "enter" the kingdom as disqualification to serve in a position of authority under Jesus in the kingdom (see 1 Corinthians 9:27). It would not have meant loss of eternal life. Even after following Jesus for perhaps more than two years, the disciples could not comprehend that Jesus would die for their sins. Their understanding of "kingdom" was earthly and messianic, reinforced by Jesus' preaching early in His ministry that the kingdom of God was at hand.

End Notes 117

4. Nicodemus (John 3:1-2) and Joseph of Arimathea (Mark 15:42-46), while believers, were slow to openly confess Jesus, perhaps due to increasing opposition and threats from Jewish leaders.
5. Young children in the Roman Empire had few rights . . . and Jesus in the following verses uses "little children" as an example of those He desires in His administration.
6. Moreover, it is likely that the faithful supporters of Jesus' ministry would have been offended had He paid the temple tax from their donations. Thus, the tax money was miraculously provided to avoid offending anyone.
7. It should be remembered that during the Milllennial reign of Christ, the earth will be populated by children born of those who became believers during the Tribulation Period and survived until Jesus' return. Thus, a great percentage of the population will be "born sinners" who need to hear the gospel of salvation, just as in this present age.
8. The common Greek verb used for "sin" (to trespass) is **harmatanō**, not **skandalizō**. Most translations improperly translate **skandalizō** in Matthew 18:6 and 18:9-10 as "to sin." This is misleading, since it fails to indicate the specific problem associated with the use of **skandalizō**.
9. If by our deeds of the flesh we cause new believers to become offended at the teachings of Christ, we are working against the kingdom . . . and are in danger of losing our earthly lives. (See Philippians 3:17-19, for example.) Death by drowning with a millstone was a form of capital punishment in the first century.
10. **Skandalizō** cannot mean "to sin" in this passage, since it would imply that eternal hell is avoided by not sinning. Nothing could be further from Biblical truth! Hell is avoided only by belief in the saving grace of Jesus. Also see Matthew 13:41, where the angels remove all that **skandalizō** and cast them into a furnace of fire.

These are the tares, those unbelievers who "took offense" at Jesus' offer of salvation.

11. See also Mark 10:35-45 and Luke 22:24-27.

Chapter 8

1. This brief discourse would have been meaningless to Judas, for example; and we see that Jesus waited until Judas had left the room before revealing the principles and importance of abiding to the remaining eleven.
2. Jesus is also the "true bread" (John 6:32) and the "true light" (John 1:9). He is "true" especially in the sense that in Him is the embodiment of all of the Old Testament types. All of them find their "true" expression and fulfillment in Him. He is also "true" in contrast to the false teaching of the scribes and Pharisees.
3. This is the last of the eight "I am" statements of Jesus in John's gospel. The "I am" statements that precede it were given in public that those who heard them might believe unto eternal life. This the only one of the eight spoken in private to the disciples He loved; and fittingly, it relates to fellowship.
4. See Deuteronomy 7:6. While Israel's <u>position</u> was attained by grace (God sovereignly chose her), the <u>condition</u> of her fellowship with the Lord and prominence among nations of the world was to be maintained by obedience (see 7:11).
5. See Matthew 13:44. Note that the "man" (Jesus) in this parable sells all that he has to purchase the treasure, but leaves it hidden in the field. Israel is still "hidden" among the nations of the world to this day, but has not been totally abandoned by God. He will revive Israel at the appointed time.
6. As a good husbandman, God watched over Jesus in His youth. This included preventing Joseph from divorcing Mary, protecting Jesus from Herod's attempt to kill him, and taking care of the family in Egypt.

End Notes 119

7. See Romans 4:3, Hebrews 11:8.
8. See Genesis 12:1-3. Compare the blessings in this passage to those of Israel in Isaiah 5:1-11. As long as Abram obediently stayed in the land, God blessed him. When he left the land, trouble arose.
9. That eternal life cannot be lost, once gained, is verified in numerous places in scripture. That "losing eternal life" is a contradiction in terms is self-evident. If eternal life could be lost, it would not be eternal to begin with.
10. See Ephesians 1:3-14.
11. Note the link between "holding fast" (***dabak***) and blessings/curses in Deuteronomy 4:1-4, 11:22-28, 28:1-68 and 30:19-20.
12. Deuteronomy 6:4ff is a good example of how Israel was to abide in the Lord. Here, as in those verses exhorting Israel to "hold fast," the promise for abiding is not eternal life, but a long life on the earth.
13. John 14:21
14. To "know Him" in this passage means to intimately know Him (or to abide in Him). The issue here is fellowship, not justification. When John says, "by this we know we are in Him," he means "we know we are <u>abiding</u> in Him," or "we know we are <u>in close fellowship</u> with Him."
15. Ephesians 4:15
16. See 2 Peter 1:5-8.
17. Jesus says in John 12:24, ". . . unless a grain of wheat falls into the ground and dies, it remains alone; but if it dies, it produces much grain." One aspect of obedience is dying to self, just as Christ laid down His life in obedience to His Father's will. In emulating Christ's example, we abide in Him.
18. In many marriages the partners never experience the depth of the relationship that God intended. God said in Genesis 2:24 for the man to leave his father and mother, and cleave (***dabak***) unto

his wife. Separation unto each other from parents establishes the marriage . . . but the joy of the relationship is in the "cleaving unto one another." As mentioned earlier, "cleaving" is the Old Testament equivalent of "abiding."

19. See the warning in Hebrews 3:12-13, where believers are to exhort one another daily, lest they become hardened in their hearts through the deceitfulness of sin.

20. In their walk through the wilderness, those who were "unclean" in the camp of the Israelites were cast <u>outside the camp</u> (Numbers 5:2-4). While they lost the privileges and blessings of being in the camp, they were still "citizens" of the nation, under the protection and guidance of God. Undoubtedly, some entered the Promised Land.

21. See Psalm 66:18, Proverbs 28:9, Mark 11:25, James 1:5-7, 4:3 and 1 Peter 3:7, for examples.

22. See Matthew 12:24, 13:22, John 15:4-5.

23. A believer's joy can be lost for a host of reasons. God's desire is that it be full to overflowing (Psalm 5:11, John 15:11, 1 John 1:4).

24. See Hebrews 6:6, 10:29. It is probable that more harm is done to the growth of the kingdom of God by wayward believers than ever imagined to be done by unbelievers.

25. While the loss of blessing and privileges in John 15:1-11 refer to this present age, a lack of abiding may affect a believer's joy and inheritance in the age to come (the Millennium). Privileges in the Millennium appear to be based on a believer's faithfulness and diligence in this current age. See Matthew 22:1-14, 25:14-29 and Luke 19:11-26. Inheritance lost by unfaithfulness is given to those who are faithful.

26. After being saved from slavery in Egypt, many Israelites worked against the purposes of God by rejecting the exhortation of Caleb and Joshua (Numbers 13:30-14:10). Note that though they died in unbelief, they were still <u>forgiven</u> (Numbers 14:20-24)! They

lost their inheritance (a privilege and a blessing), but not their covenant relationship.

27. Philippians 3:18-19
28. Especially notice Hebrews 6:7-8, where "burning" is the result of a believer who has fallen so far from grace that it is impossible for fellow believers to bring him to repentance (see 6:4-6).
29. See Genesis 13:12.
30. See 1 Corinthians 3:12-15, 2 Corinthians 5:3, 10 and 1 John 2:28.
31. For a more detailed explanation of "weeping and gnashing of teeth", see Chapter 5 – "Robes and Wedding Garments."
32. Some have used Matthew 7:16-20 to support the idea that a believer's justification can be verified by his fruit (or lack thereof). However, this passage applies strictly to identifying false teachers, not believers. Other passages, such as Matthew 3:10 and 12:33, should similarly be understood. It is clear from the gospels and many of the epistles that a believer is capable of forfeiting his "place in the vine;" losing the ability to produce fruit.
33. Also see Deuteronomy 4:23-24.

APPENDIX A

How to enhance the quality of your eternal life

Verse	Characteristics	Consequences
Matthew 5:17-20	Obey the commandments and teach them	You will be greatest in the kingdom
Matthew 10:32	Confess God before men (is a good witness; a faithful disciple) • Become a servant like his Master (10:25) • Be willing to be demeaned for the sake of his Master (10:27) • Openly speak the word of God (10:28) • Be willing to suffer persecution and death (10:28) • Love Jesus more than your own family (10:37) • Love Jesus more than yourself (10:39)	You will be confessed (recommended) before the Father
Matthew 18:2-4	Humble yourself as a little child	You will be great in the kingdom of heaven
Matthew 19:21	Forsake the world to follow Jesus	You will have (already has) treasure in heaven

Verse	Characteristics	Consequences
Matthew 20:1-16	Live by grace (trust in the goodness of the landowner)	You will be honored; be first; experience joy
Matthew 25:14-23	Be faithful, fruitful, and make a "profit" for our Lord	You will have an administrative position in the kingdom
Luke 10:25-28	Love God and neighbor as yourself	You will have an inheritance in eternal life
Luke 16:1-13	Lay up for the life to come; be faithful with what you have	You will have an abundant entrance into the kingdom
Luke 22:28-30	Continue in Jesus' trials	You will sit at table with Christ, and rule with Christ
Romans 8:17	Suffer with Christ	You will be a joint heir with Christ
1 Corinthians 3:14	Build your life in Christ with enduring materials	You will be rewarded
1 Corinthians 9:24-25	Run the race so as to win the prize	You will receive an imperishable crown
Galatians 6:8	Sow to the Spirit	You will reap in eternity
Colossians 3:23-25	Do whatever you do as to the Lord	You will receive the reward of your inheritance
1 Timothy 6:11-19	Pursue righteousness, godliness, faith, love, etc.	You will store up a good foundation for the age to come

Appendix A

Verse	Characteristics	Consequences
2 Timothy 2:12	Endure trials	You will reign with Christ
2 Peter 1:6-10	Exhibit self-control, perseverance, godliness, kindness, love	You will be fruitful; have an abundant entrance into the kingdom
1 John 2:28	Abide in Jesus	You will face Jesus with confidence when He returns
Revelation 2:7	Lead an overcoming life	You will be allowed to eat from the "tree of life"
Revelation 2:10	Be faithful under persecution unto death	You will be given the crown of life
Revelation 2:17	Overcome the temptations of life	You will be given a new name by Christ
Revelation 2:25-26	Hold fast and overcome temptations	You will be given the responsibility of ruling; and the morning star
Revelation 3:5	Be watchful; hold fast and overcome	You will be given a radiant garment; confessed before the Father
Revelation 3:11	Hold fast to the faith; lead an overcoming life	You will be given a crown, a new name; be a pillar in God's temple

APPENDIX B

How to diminish the quality of your eternal life

Verse	Characteristics	Consequences
Matthew 5:17-20	Dismiss the commandments and teach others to do the same	You will be least in the kingdom
Matthew 8:11-12	Fail to exhibit a life of faith	You will be cast outside the banquet hall; to weep and grieve
Matthew 10:33	Lead a lifestyle that "denies" Christ	You will be "denied" before the Father
Matthew 20:1-16	Live legalistically	You will lose honor, blessing and joy; and be "last" in the kingdom
Matthew 22:11-14	Fail to be prepared for the wedding banquet	You will not be welcome at the wedding banquet
Matthew 24:51	Beat fellow servants; drink/eat with drunkards	You will be "cut in pieces" and have the same portion as hypocrites
Matthew 25:24-30	Be lazy and wicked; be unprofitable for Christ	You will lose your reward, joy; be unwelcome at the wedding banquet
Mark 8:38	Act ashamed of Christ and His words	Christ will be ashamed of you when He returns

Appendix B

Verse	Characteristics	Consequences
Luke 12:16-21	Live a worldly, selfish life	You will be called a fool by God; and have no treasure in heaven
Luke 15:11-32	Live a riotous, worldly life	You will lose your inheritance
Luke 16:11-12	Live an unfaithful life; serve mammon	You will lose what would have been your own
1Corinthians 3:15	Build your life in Christ with poor quality materials	Your works will be burned up; you will lose your reward
1Corinthians 3:16-17	Corrupt the temple of God (the life you have been given)	Your rewards in heaven will be corrupted
1Corinthians 9:27	Lead an undisciplined life	You will be disqualified
2Corinthians 5:2-4	Fail to walk by faith or do worthwhile things for Christ	You will find yourself "naked" before Christ
2Corinthians 5:10	Do worthless things with your life	You will receive from God according to your worthless deeds
Galatians 5:19-21	Live according to the flesh	You will lose your inheritance in the coming kingdom
Galatians 6:7-8	Sow to the flesh	You will reap corruption of the quality of your eternal life
Ephesians 5:3-5	Live according to the flesh; become a son of disobedience	You will experience wrath, and lose your inheritance

Verse	Characteristics	Consequences
Ephesians 5:5-6	Live a fornicating, covetous, idolatrous, fruitless life	You will experience wrath, and lose your inheritance
Philippians 3:18-19	Walk according to the flesh; set your mind on earthly things	You will experience shame and destruction
Colossians 2:18-19	Engage in false worship, do not hold fast to Christ	You will be cheated out of your reward
Colossians 3:25	Be disobedient; do wrong	You will be repaid in kind; and given no partiality
Hebrews 2:2-3	Neglect your salvation	You will not escape God's justice
Hebrews 10:26-31	Willfully sin; trample the Son of God underfoot; insult the Spirit	You will be repaid for your deeds; a frightful experience
Hebrews 12:16-17	Live like Esau, treat your inheritance as a common thing	You will lose your inheritance and joy; you will have no recourse
1John 2:28	Fail to abide in Jesus	You will be ashamed at the Lord's coming
Revelation 3:3	Fail to be watchful or to hold fast to the faith; don't repent	You will be unprepared at the Lord's coming

www.ingramcontent.com/pod-product-compliance
Lightning Source LLC
LaVergne TN
LVHW051524070426
835507LV00023B/3281